CONTEMPORARY
SIOUX
PAINTING

An exhibition organized by the
Indian Arts and Crafts Board
of the United States
Department of the Interior

CONTEMPORARY SIOUX PAINTING

Exhibition released through the

SIOUX INDIAN MUSEUM AND CRAFTS CENTER,

Rapid City, South Dakota, a cultural

facility administered and operated by

the Indian Arts and Crafts Board of the

U.S. Department of the Interior, in

cooperation with the City of Rapid City.

Catalogue of the exhibition published by
the TIPI SHOP, INC., Rapid City, South Dakota, 1970.

Library of Congress Catalogue Card Number 70-119593

Printed in the United States of America by Simpson's Creative Printers,

Rapid City, South Dakota.

Cover. 14 OSCAR HOWE: *Medicine Man.* (1962)

FOREWORD AND ACKNOWLEDGEMENTS

During the past few decades the increasing interest of contemporary Indian artists in extending their training and experience into the latest and most innovative forms of painting evolving in the United States today, has resulted in the creation of a growing body of experimental works of art which explore new depths of the Native American artistic genius.

Until very recently however, there has been little public awareness of the increasing variety and vitality of the contemporary achievement by modern Indian artists in the United States.

Of particular interest is the rapid and brilliant evolution of painting by artists of Sioux descent during the 20th century, the contemporary manifestation of an enduring legacy of indigenous North American Indian art. This artistic tradition, in fact, began over 200 years ago, when the western branches of the Sioux undertook an important cultural development, born of an inspiring and demanding way of life as big-game hunters on the High Plains of North America. As the temporary guardians of this impressive cultural legacy, and in the same adventuresome spirit as that of their innovative ancestors, the 20th century artists represented in this exhibition, "Contemporary Sioux Painting", are projecting their native genius to new pinacles of achievement in the modern world.

This exhibition originated as a research project undertaken by the Indian Arts and Crafts Board of the U.S. Department of the Interior through the Sioux Indian Museum and Crafts Center in Rapid City, South Dakota, a cultural facility operated and administered by the Indian Arts and Crafts Board.

"Contemporary Sioux Painting" comprises the first historical survey and evaluation of the varied and brilliant development of painting by artists of Sioux descent, from the turn of the century to the present. The paintings comprising the exhibition are from the invaluable Indian art collections of the Indian Arts and Crafts Board, selected primarily from the collections maintained at the Board's Sioux Indian Museum and Crafts Center in Rapid City, South Dakota, which are an important resource of the U.S. Department of the Interior.

It is a special pleasure for the Indian Arts and Crafts Board to introduce this exhibition to the extensive audience it will reach while circulating to museums and art galleries in the United States.

The initial tour of the exhibition was made possible by the generous cooperation of the South Dakota Arts Council, which has undertaken the responsibility for arranging showings of "Contemporary Sioux Painting" throughout the state of South Dakota, where over two-thirds of the Sioux population live today.

The Indian Arts and Crafts Board is most appreciative of the assistance received from the artists and their families, who have provided valuable biographical information on the artists represented in the exhibition. For the kind cooperation of the many Indian individuals who have graciously shared with the Indian Arts and Crafts Board their knowledge, recollections, and photographs of the earlier artists of the present century, we wish to express our deep gratitude.

Vincent Price
Chairman
Indian Arts and Crafts Board

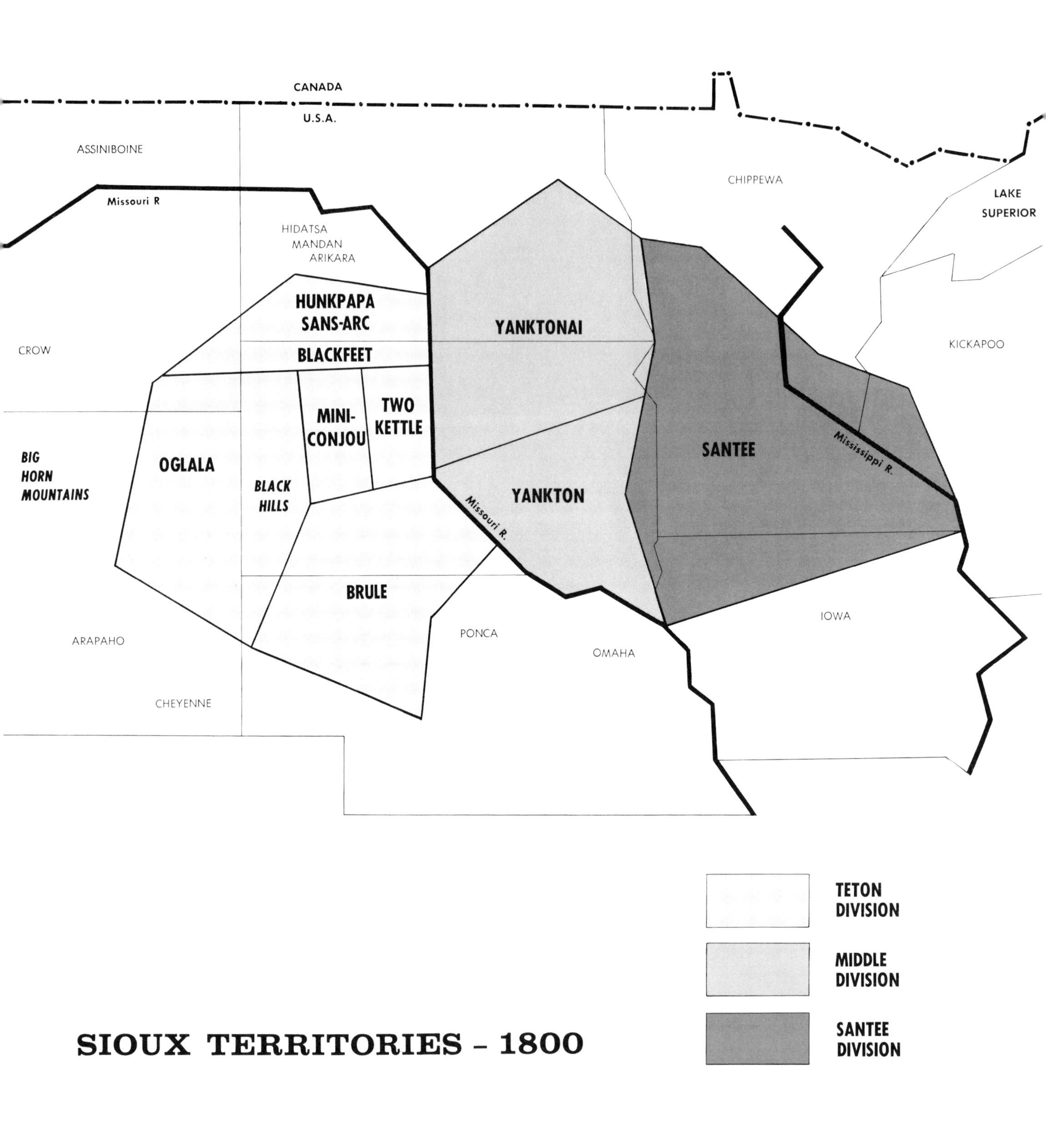

SIOUX TERRITORIES – 1800

INTRODUCTION

The unique and enduring development of Sioux painting in the United States is considered to have begun during the early 18th century when several bands of the Sioux emigrated from their ancestral homelands in the forested areas near Lake Superior, gradually drifting to new territories to the west, ultimately to adjust to an adventuresome, completely new way of life as big-game hunters on the High Plains. In their new hunting territories on the Plains the western Sioux took up pursuit of the immense herds of American bison – more commonly known as the buffalo – which freely roamed throughout what was then a vast, natural grassland of central North America. As a result of their move to the High Plains, and their adaptation to life in a new environment, the western branches of the Sioux naturally forged an important series of new art styles and forms, among which certainly the most impressive were their painting arts. These arts they intensely developed to great variety and stature during the tumultuous events of the following century – first as they gained territory, power and influence as one of the most vital of the hunter-warrior societies of the Plains, and secondly, during the period which witnessed the confrontation of their indigenous society by the overwhelming thrust and impetus of a modern nation pursuing its own destiny in the New World.

The Sioux reaction and resistance to an abrupt adjustment to the modern, technological age was natural and inevitable, but in the process revealed that the vitality and adventuresomeness of Sioux character was always ready to receive fresh stimuli. For well over the past 250 years – from the time they forged their own frontiers on the High Plains, to their present-day participation in the variety of experiences in the contemporary society of the United States – their creative impulse has never faltered.

Today over 55,000 individuals of Sioux descent live on or near reservation areas, established during the latter half of the 19th century, which are broadly scattered among five states – North and South Dakota, Montana, Minnesota and Nebraska *(see map page 21)*.

Although widely dispersed, the total Sioux population comprises the second largest Indian tribe now living in the United States. The majority of the Sioux reservations are located in the state of South Dakota, and their residents are primarily comprised of descendants of the western branches of the tribe – the Teton, the Yankton and the Yanktonai – who have developed today, as in the past, a remarkable number of accomplished and inventive artists.

In recognition of their importance to the artistic production of the United States today, it is of considerable significance that a surprising spectrum of contemporary artists of western Sioux descent have found renewed inspiration for their works in the impressive tribal heritage of rich and varied forms of painting. A full appreciation of the contemporary achievement requires some consideration not only of the development of 19th century Sioux painting arts, but also of the unique historic development of the tribe itself, all of which has stimulated much of the content and expression for the contemporary paintings presented in this exhibition.

THE EXPANSION AND CULTURAL DIVERSIFICATION OF THE SIOUX DURING THE 18TH AND 19TH CENTURIES

The Sioux belong to a group of tribes speaking related languages, comprising what has become known as the Siouan language stock, one of the largest of the several major language families of aboriginal North America. Scholars of the pre-Columbian period in North America believe the early Siouan-speaking peoples originated in the vicinity of the Ohio River Valley where they were forced from the region by a northeastern movement of other pre-Columbian peoples, which dispersed the Siouan tribes in several directions – some groups drifting further to the east, while others migrated westward. The Sioux of later history were among the largest of the several Siouan-speaking groups to move west, ultimately occupying a territory west of the Great Lakes. The tribe was divided into several bands, and in their native tongue called themselves DAKOTA, meaning "Friends" or "Allies". Their tribal enemies, the Chippewa, however, referred to them as "Nadoweisiw-eg", meaning "Snakes" or "Adders", which the French, to whom the Chippewa were allied, later corrupted to the now more familiar and widely accepted name, SIOUX.

When the Sioux were first mentioned by white explorers – about 1640 – the tribe was still consolidated in an area west of Lake Superior, where their culture was similar to that of other Woodland tribes of the region. According to the tribe's legendary origins, the Sioux were then organized into seven major bands, or "Council Fires". During the last decades of the 17th century, partly under pressure exerted by the Chippewa whom the French had armed with guns, the Teton, the Yankton, and the Yanktonai bands of the Sioux had begun a gradual, westward penetration into new territories.

This expansion by several of the tribal bands into new ecological areas naturally resulted in the development of important cultural as well as dialectic differences among the Sioux and three great divisions of the tribe soon came to be recognized.

The eastern, or SANTEE division of the Sioux, speaking the *Dakota* dialect, retained four of the original bands – the Mdewakanton, Wahpekute, Sisseton and Wahpeton. The Santee remained in the traditional homelands west of the Great Lakes, a region comprising forests and lakes, interspersed by patches of prairie lands. Here the Santee continued the ancestral pattern of life common to other Woodland Indians of the region, living in bark-covered dwellings and practicing a mixed economy of hunting, fishing, gathering and horticulture. In their arts the Santee produced garments and implements which resembled those of their Algonquian neighbors to the east and north, sharing their preferences for decorative motifs of floral and curvilinear designs, which, in time, were to stand in striking contrast to the new arts to be developed by their western brethren.

By the end of the 18th century, the three bands moving to the west had overcome and routed a variety of other tribes in their path and had indisputedly established for themselves vast new territories. In the process the western bands developed into two additional divisions of the tribe, the Yankton and Yanktonai bands forming one division, controlling territories between the lands of the Santee westward to the Missouri River, with the Teton band pushing further westward to the High Plains where they were to constitute a third division of the tribe. Indeed, during the 18th century the Sioux developed into one of the largest and most powerful tribes in North America, with the total extent of territories under control of the respective tribal divisions extending from the Mississippi River in the east to the Black Hills in the west, with the nomadic Tetons roving and hunting as far west as the Big Horn Mountains.

During their conquest of new territories the two western divisions of the tribe were naturally exposed to innumerable creative stimuli – the differing natural resources of the new ecological environments into which they moved, the striking life ways and customs of the foreign tribes which they defeated or befriended, as well as the technological impact of the horse and the gun which had been introduced by the white man – all of which in time promoted the development of new arts and fashions among the westward moving Sioux.

In their new domains encompassing lands on the eastern banks of the Missouri River, the Yankton and Yanktonai bands, soon speaking their distinctive dialect, *Nakota*, formed the MIDDLE division of the tribe. Here the Yankton and Yanktonai adjusted to a varied economy similar to that long established by earlier peoples inhabiting the area, combining fishing and river-bottom horticulture with, in the spring and fall of each year, great bison hunting expeditions to the High Plains west of the Missouri River. Although the Yankton and Yanktonai thus became dependent upon the bison as an important source of food, unlike their Teton relatives who moved to the High Plains, they did not adjust to a completely nomadic hunting existence. While the portable tipi was commonly used as a dwelling by both the Yankton and Yanktonai, the latter also adapted to life in small villages of earth lodges – wooden-beamed, earth-covered structures – such as those inhabited by their Missouri River neighbors, the Arikaras, Mandan and Hidatsas.

In their dress the Yankton and Yanktonai bands adopted the fringed buckskin garments common to all Plains tribes, but were generally more conservative in the embellishment of their dress than the Teton. Reflecting their intermediate positions in the tribe, in their decorative arts they continued to employ both the floral and curvilinear Woodland designs of the Santee, while also adapting to the geometric designs favored by the Teton and other tribes of the High Plains. As their economy did not demand constant nomadism, their close relationship with other semisedentary tribes in the Missouri River area prompted them to also produce some pottery and basketry, arts which their wholly nomadic cousins, the Tetons, were to eschew for practical reasons.

The most phenomenal cultural revolution within the tribe was undertaken by the TETON band, which, by the middle of the 18th century, had boldly crossed the Missouri River and began pushing their frontiers across the High Plains, eventually gaining the rich treasures of the Black Hills – the wintering grounds of the bison, a prime source of building materials, and long regarded as a place of great religious significance by Indian peoples of the area. In these new lands, which they soon brought under their control, the Teton were destined to achieve a most remarkable and swift ascendance to power among the Indian tribes dwelling on the northern Plains.

A vital and aggressive people, the adventuresome Tetons not only quickly adjusted to the rigors of big-game hunting on the High Plains, but also successfully prospered in their achievement, developing a large population which soon exceeded in number all other divisions of the tribe combined. Soon speaking their own dialect, *Lakota*, the Teton in fact developed as a major division of the Sioux, and were themselves organized into seven important bands – the Oglala, Brule, Miniconjou, Two Kettle, Hunkpapa, Blackfeet and Sans Arc – names which during the following century were to become en-

A PARFLECHE.
Sioux 19th century.
Painted rawhide,
13 x 25".
Gift of Mrs.
Orpha Haxby (1032)

graved forever in the history of the eventful expansion and consolidation of the United States.

In adapting to a hunting economy almost wholly dependent upon a single animal – the bison – the Teton shared with other hunting tribes of the Plains an exciting and often precarious existence in a difficult and demanding environment.

In taking up a completely nomadic life, the Teton naturally adapted to living in the portable tipi, a conical-shaped tent-like structure, ideally suited for ease of transport as well as for providing protection against the relentless elements of the Plains.

In their dress the Teton adopted the fringed buckskin garments, decorated with bold geometric motifs in quill or bead appliques, as commonly worn by all the nomadic hunting tribes dwelling on the High Plains. As they grew prosperous in their exploitation of the bison, they began to lavish ever richer embellishments upon their possessions, becoming ostentatiously proudful of their magnificence.

The timing and eventful circumstances surrounding the Tetons' emergence as a nomadic hunting tribe on the High Plains, in combination with their adventuresome, aggressive and competitive character as a people, enabled them to so boldly assert the creative and positive aspects of their culture, to keep at bay numerous enemy tribes, and to successfully conquer a severe and relentless environment.

At the time of the Teton's migrations to the area, the High Plains – comprising one of the largest ecological areas of the North American continent – stretched as an immense, unbroken "sea of grass", extending from the heartland of Canada in the north to the Rio Grande River in the south, and bordered on the west by the foothills of the Rocky Mountain chain with an eastern boundary paralleling the prairie lands west of the Mississippi River.

The entire region was one through which Indian hunters had roamed from prehistoric times, undaunted by the varied climatic conditions of the area, including blizzards, drought, floods, tornadoes, dust storms, and searing heat.

Like the earlier peoples migrating to the area, the Teton were attracted by the multitude of natural resources available in the Plains environment. Of major importance was the abundance of long and short stemmed grasses providing an immense natural pasture for the roving herds of bison, as well as antelope, deer and other animals, from which the Plains Indians obtained food and raw materials for the manufacture of clothing, implements and shelter. Throughout the area, the variety of vegetation also provided food, dyes, medicines, and building materials.

When they first emerged upon the Plains, the Teton traversed the region on foot in search of wild game, utilizing the dog as their only beast of burden, at best a precarious and difficult existence. Within a short time of their migration to the area, however, their life was quickly and dramatically revolutionized by their adaptation to use of the horse.

As early as the 16th century, the horse had been introduced to the North American Indian by Spanish settlers in the Southwest, and, during the 18th century, appeared on the north-central Plains through intertribal contacts. Called SHUNKA WAKAN, or "Holy Dog", by the Teton, the horse brought a new tempo to their nomadic life, providing a vastly improved method for hunting bison and allowing a swifter and more effective means of moving camp in pursuit of the roaming herds. These two animals – the horse and the bison – influenced virtually all aspects of Teton life and were destined to give a distinctive definition to their arts, which has persisted to the present day.

During the hunt and in all camp activities, cooperative effort and sharing were of prime importance. Despite the aggressive and competitive aspect of Sioux character, as a necessary principle of life within the tribe generosity was an abiding ideal and, in fact, social status was achieved through the amounts of food, horses, and possessions which were given away. Political organization was highly democratic. Certain of the most honored and respected men, the WAKINCUZAS, or "Wise Ones", served as advisers by the consent of the people, with dignity, wisdom, and fairness required attributes of their positions. Special societies or fraternities of a military and ceremonial character were called upon to police and maintain order during large bison hunts and on other important tribal occasions.

Religion and ceremony pervaded every aspect of Sioux life. The most important religious ceremony was the Sun Dance, observed each summer, when all the wandering camps reconvened to perform the sacred rites which assured the renewal of the bison and reaffirmed the well-being of the people.

In Sioux religion, WAKAN TANKA is the all-encompassing concept of a controlling power, or series of powers, pervading the universe. The aid of these powers was sought by western Sioux men through induced visions, calling upon all the recognized mythical creatures, the heavenly bodies, and all on earth and in the waters. Through a visionary experience, any one of the forces of nature – the moon, stars, a hawk, or bison – could become a supernatural helper to an individual in all life's endeavors – the hunt, combat, and even the playing of simple sports or games.

B ROBE. Reconstruction (1963) of 19th century "feathered circle" design, by Herman Red Elk, Yanktonai Sioux. Painted bison hide, maximum dimensions: 71 x 77". (70.3.3)

In a life dominated by the spirit of the chase, it was natural for an intense competition to develop between the Plains tribes, and an elaborate system of warfare flowered. As a means of acquiring worldly goods through booty, as well as for exerting tribal power in the conquest of new hunting grounds, combat was also an exciting way of trying to get the better of one's opponents, thereby earning status as a brave warrior.

Thus, to their intense esteem of self and nation, the western Sioux also brought innovation, courage and adaptability, by which they became the most notably successful people to fully realize a rich and rewarding life offered by the natural resources of the High Plains.

THE FORMS AND DEVELOPMENT OF SIOUX PAINTING DURING THE 19TH CENTURY

By the beginning of the 19th century the western Sioux had adapted to use of the full spectrum of arts developed within the larger patterns of culture which they shared in common with other bison hunting tribes dwelling on the High Plains. Their successful exploitation of the resources of the Plains environment soon brought new wealth which was reflected by a florescence of their arts.

An economy based almost entirely upon bison hunting led naturally to the development of arts which made extensive use of the hides of animals, one of the most valuable by-products of the hunt. Practically everything they produced for their needs – container forms, garments, ritual equipment for ceremonies, implements for the hunt or battle, even their dwelling, the tipi – were ingeniously fashioned from the hides and skins of animals. Ideally suited for their nomadic existence, objects and implements produced of animal skins were nonbreakable, light weight and readily folded and packed for ease of transport by horse and travois. Hides were processed by two methods, either untreated rawhide for objects which required some stability and retention of form, as required for containers and shields, or soft-dressed skins as employed for production of garments and tipis.

Both methods of hide preparation provided excellent surfaces for decoration, and the urge to beautify their surroundings resulted in the development of innumerable decorative and expressive concepts. Indeed, practically every object or item produced was richly decorated, either by quill, bead or paint. As painting was ideally suited to the decoration of both rawhide and soft-dressed skins, the western Sioux took full advantage for self-expression through this medium.

One of their most ancient arts, painting remained, throughout the 19th century, an important artistic medium among the western Sioux and was in fact brought to new heights of aesthetic and expressive achievement.

Initially, pigments were necessarily prepared by grinding to powdered form a variety of natural earth substances, like ochres or lignites. While these early paints were relatively few and muted in tone, by the late 18th century a brighter palette had already been achieved through a variety of dry pigments introduced by white traders – including Chinese vermillion, as well as greens and blues. Thus, the favored colors in classic works by the western Sioux display a vivid combination of red, yellows, blue and green. With no attempt to reproduce naturalistic hues, color was utilized for its primal, abstract value in creating well-ordered, effective compositions.

Compositions for paintings on soft-dressed skins were often laid out with a sharpened wedge of horn or wood, simply sketching designs or figures by pressure and abrasion on the surface of the skin, while geometric designs on rawhide were often laid out with strategically located spots or guidelines of color, produced by sticks dipped in wet pigment. Broader areas of color to develop the finished composition were then applied by use of shaved pieces of porous bison leg bone, dipped in liquid pigments. A separate bone "brush" was used for each color. To assure their adhesion to the hide or skin being decorated, pigments were mixed with glutinous substances obtained from boiling hide scrapings or beaver tails.

Despite the obvious simplicity of the methods and materials, the full import of the western Sioux achievement in painting is clearly revealed by the diversity of objects upon which compositions were created, including the rectangular formats offered by rawhide containers, the circular format of shields, as well as the irregular shapes of large robes, the latter comprised of the entire hide of a bison with appendages of legs and head intact. In addition, compositions were also ingeniously created, for viewing in the round, on three dimensional objects like cylindrical rawhide cases, and perhaps most impressive of all, on the exterior coverings of large, conical-shaped tipis.

For each of these special objects schematic standards were established for the compositions to be created in their decoration. Most importantly, a natural specialization defined by the artist's sex and role in society determined the type of object to be decorated, and the

C ROBE. Reconstruction (1963) of 19th century "border and box" design, by Herman Red Elk, Yanktonai Sioux. Painted bison hide, maximum dimensions: 83 x 86". (70.3.2)

stylistic mode to be employed in executing the decoration.

Thus in their important roles as hunters, warriors and the keepers of vital religious observances, men assumed the production of compositions containing life forms as well as the depiction of supernatural beings. Life forms were most frequently painted upon bison robes and tipis, while images representing supernatural beings were executed on shields and other implements of ritual significance. By striking contrast, women as the keepers of households, in meeting their primary responsibilities for the forthright beautification of the more intimate possessions of the family circle, created bold, decorative compositions comprised of geometric elements.

As women varied their mastery of geometric compositions by practicing a wide range of media – preferring sewn applique techniques, utilizing beads or porcupine quills, for decorating soft skin articles such as garments – their work in painting was therefore primarily directed to decorating those items for which that medium was more practical.

In this respect their most impressive painted compositions were created in the decoration of two major types of objects, hard-surfaced rawhide containers, for which sewn applique techniques were inappropriate, as well as on bison robes, requiring compositions covering a large and expansive surface. Each of these objects was decorated with distinctive compositions.

For instance, schematic concepts for paintings on the rigidly rectangular fields offered by rawhide containers were always directed to bilaterally symmetrical compositions of bold, geometric motifs which filled the entire field (Illustration A).

However, on large bison robes, compositions of a more expansive nature were painted. Of the several types of geometric compositions created on robes by the Plains Indian, two basic patterns were preferred by the Sioux. One of these patterns featured a large central medallion composed of concentric rows of regularly spaced units, each unit comprised of two triangles flanking a rectangular bar (Illustration B).

A more complex composition was required for creation of the second most favored geometric pattern for robes. The basic concept of this composition, which suggests a schematic, abstracted depiction of a bison, comprised a large rectangular motif situated to one side of an unpainted central field which, in turn, was enclosed by an ornate border in a rectangular configuration (Illustration C). In both of these basic patterns the painted areas were executed in various colors defining intricate, interlocking geometric elements which, in the overall work, created a strikingly rich visual effect.

The representational forms of painting created by men also were of several distinctive types, and for the most part were vividly expressive of their vital activities as hunters and warriors.

A first major category includes compositions which were primarily religious in nature and were painted on objects created for service in ritual observances to propitiate beneficient supernatural spirits, upon which the individual depended for his safety and well-being.

All Plains Indian men undertook a vision quest, requiring a period of fasting in a remote wilderness area. If successful in this quest, the individual was visited, in trance, by some spirit of nature or other imaginary supernatural being which provided gifts of protective charms or formulas, including ritual songs and dances to be observed in the future to assure the continued efficacy of the spirit's aid.

Paintings representing a supernatural helper were most commonly executed on circular shields, which were employed for ritualistic use as a protective charm in battle. Reflecting their serious and vital significance, depictions of supernatural assistants were wrought with austere and emphatic imagery, generally in compositions with stark, bilateral symmetry. As required by the nature of a specific subject, or by the complexity of the artist's intent, these paintings ranged from straightforward representational renderings of the spirit's earthly form to highly subjective symbolic abstractions, and often to an artful combination of both modes (Illustration D).

Depictions of supernatural helpers also were produced as part of the ritual equipment for WOTAWE, or "medicine bundles", employed by shamen for such special purposes as curing, controlling the weather, or promoting the supply of bison (Illustration E).

A second major category of representational compositions were devoted to paintings of a more frankly secular, as well as literary, nature. The subjects of these works were directed to depictions of battle and other daring exploits by individual warriors.

In the highly competitive and democratic society of the western Sioux, status was gained by the society's acknowledgement of – and continued regard for – one's courageous and daring deeds. To proclaim and promote recognition of their personal valor and accomplishment, warriors were prompted to create visual records and documents of their achievements.

The complexity of such painted subjects required a sizeable format for effective rendering, as many warrior records were epic in content. These visual narratives were therefore most commonly painted on frequently-used articles of dress as large bison robes worn by the warrior, as well as on more monumental structures as

D SHIELD COVER. Belonged to Short Bull, a Brule Sioux. Late 19th century. Canvas, painted with powdered pigments and crayons, diameter 17". Anonymous gift. (69.10.1)

the exterior covering of the tipi, owned by the warrior's wife, or on dew-cloth linings hung around the interior of the tipi. On all of these items the narratives were of course readily available for public reference.

As representational depictions of actual exploits, the compositions were remarkable, both for their aesthetic quality and as highly successful forms of autobiography.

The overall composition of a narrative work generally filled the entire field upon which the painting was executed. The composition was conceived as a more or less complex series of individual vignettes, each documenting specific actions and detailing significant fact. In this manner, the composition was generally directed to expressing either a series of events widely separated by time and place, or to conveying various actions, often directly interrelated, which were taken during a single important epic event. To a people with only an oral literature, an invaluable and impressive amount of information could be extracted by effectively scanning the total composition of a pictorial narrative (Illustration F).

As the objectives of the narrative style were directed primarily to documenting the valorous subjects of battle or horse stealing, the artist adhered to only the most essential images required to convey the message – man and horse. To emphasize through an effective pictorial means the actions and events to be featured, these figures were always depicted in profile, granting full opportunity to graphically represent any detail deemed essential. All other detail such as background or landscape setting was naturally eliminated.

All figures or groups of images were drawn in a flat, highly stylized manner, perspective and volume sensitively suggested by an ingenious variety of bold but elemental devices, such as by overlapping planes and, in the aesthetically best works, by the subtle grouping and interrelationship of integral parts of the composition.

The narrative style witnessed intense development during the 19th century as a variety of new stimuli reached the Plains Sioux, triggered by increased encounters with the white man. The artist however, wavered not at all in the basic pictorial principles of the narrative style, so long as he produced under motivations generated by his own society.

Early 19th century works are executed in an archaic manner featuring extremely simplified, often static images which are little more than symbolic of man and beast. In time images conveyed more action, with lively horses presented in the "flying gallop", and with figures of warriors often containing a wealth of descriptive detail, accurately recording the changing fashions resulting from the increasing ostentation of dress and personal adornment.

A third important form of representational paintings were calendrical histories of individual tribal bands. Commonly called "winter counts", these works were comprised of a continuous series of images, each image representing an important event which marked an annual period in the band's history. The subjects for annual entries were chosen in council or by common agreement, and the record's preservation was entrusted to an individual keeper.

Generally the entries in calendrical histories were painted in an extremely elementary manner, and their simplified figures therefore resemble those of the archaic pictographic work of the early narrative style, with which these works are closely related. First produced on hides, as the originals wore out, the record was renewed on a freshly prepared hide or, during the latter 19th century, were transferred to paper notebooks (Illustration G).

These records are the only evidence of any practice among the North American Indian to compile a systematic historical document of his people, and it is of interest here to note that the keeping of these calendrical records were unique to the Teton Sioux and the Kiowa of the High Plains.

The 19th century painting arts of the western Sioux were impressive and remarkable for the variety of their concepts and for the stature of their aesthetic achievement. Indeed, throughout the century, among the most vital and creative arts of the far western frontier were indeed those of the American Indian. In the depictions wrought by the western Sioux, the march of the century is clearly revealed, so vividly recorded as the white man at last made his appearance in the personal narratives painted by the warrior-artist. These works of art stand in mute testament to the fateful upheaval with which the artist's society was ultimately confronted.

To be sure, the relentless expansion of the modern age was pushing its frontiers across the entire globe. In North America, as the 19th century dawned, the United States had gained its first overland sighting of the Pacific, only to be distracted and finally shaken by the ideological conflict of a great civil war, yet emerging with a burning desire for consolidation of what it considered to be its natural boundaries – a national ideal not unlike that of the westward moving Sioux a century before.

Developments during the 19th century brought increasing numbers of white men to the western hunting domains of the Sioux – explorers, traders, and finally settlers and the military. As interactions between the two peoples intensified, enthusiasm for the white man's trade goods was ultimately overshadowed by concern over his increased intrusion upon hunting grounds. During the latter decades of the century armed conflicts oc-

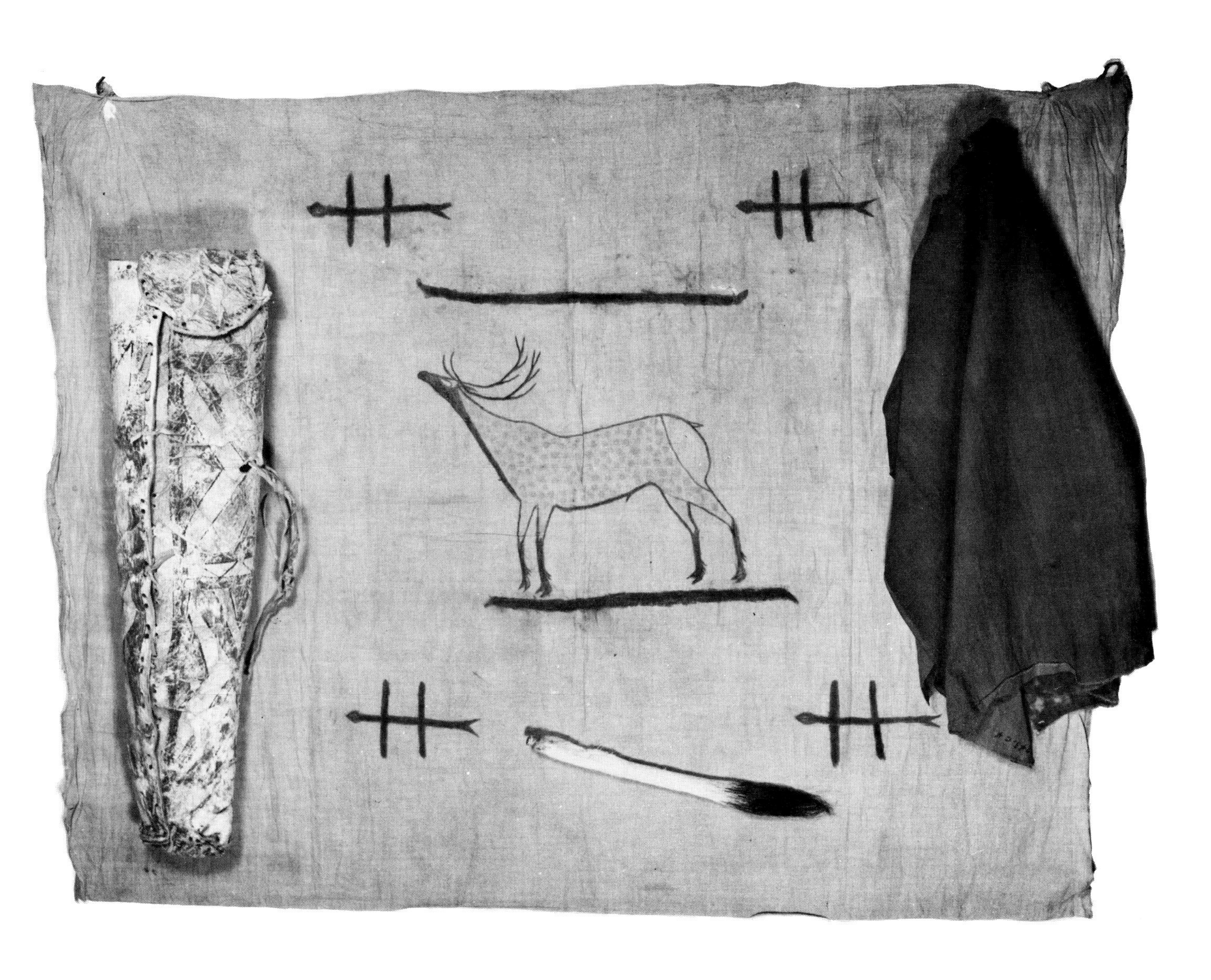

E WOTAWE, or "medicine bundle". Belonged to Sitting Bull, a Hunkpapa Sioux. 19th century. Painted muslin, 25 x 33"; shown with rawhide container (left) and other contents of the bundle. (1243)

F ROBE. Reconstruction (1966) of 19th century "warrior's narrative" composition, by Herman Red Elk, Yanktonai Sioux. Painted bison hide, maximum dimensions: 94 x 92". (67.4.2) OPPOSITE PAGE: Detail of robe.

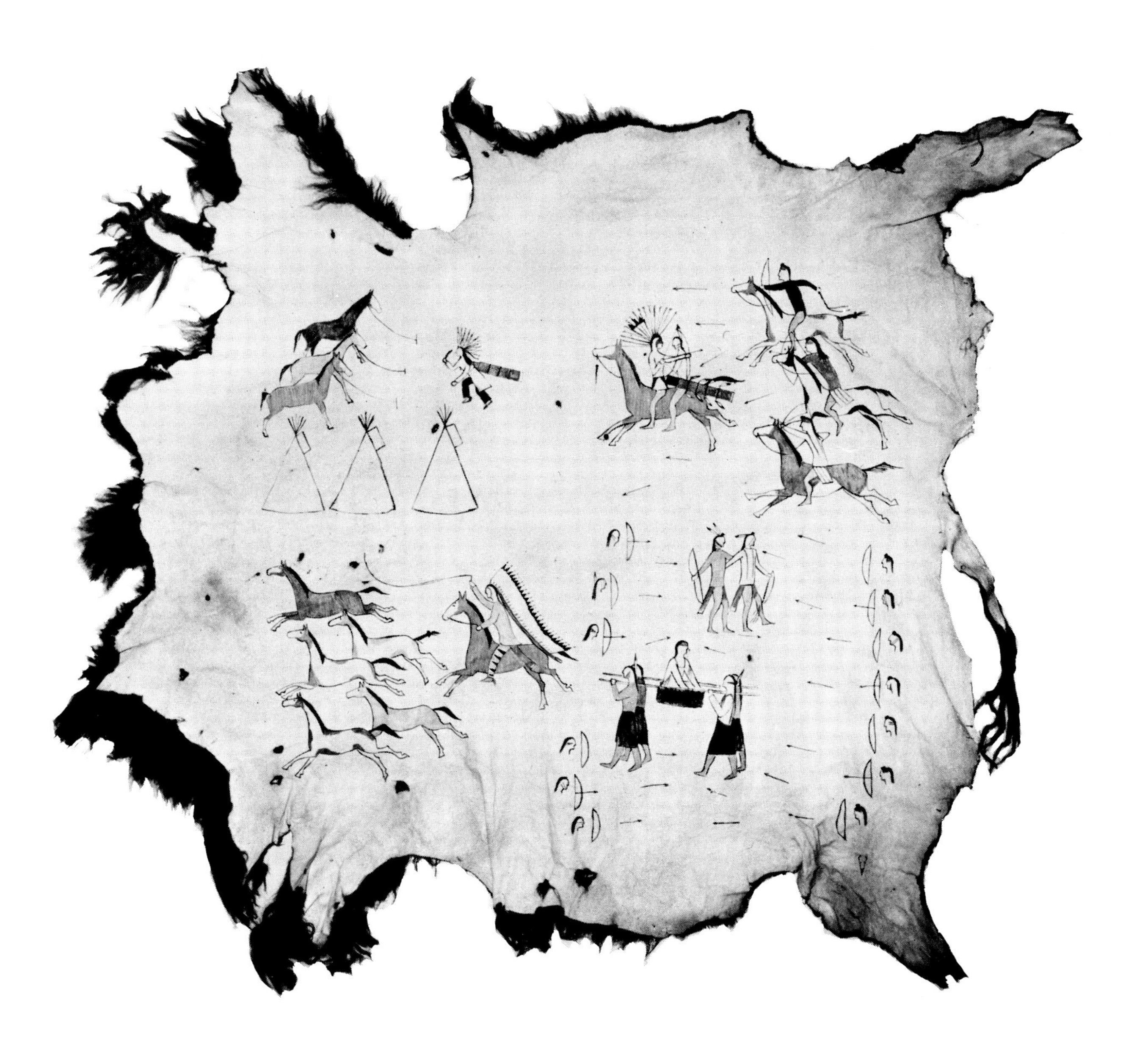

curred, the bison were depleted, and the various bands were ultimately settled upon reservations, dependent upon the aid of the government. While the period was indeed a dark one, by the close of the century the western Sioux were resolutely set about reordering their lives to the measure of the times, gradually adjusting to the concepts of the white man's customs and clothing and, with the bison gone, searching for a new economic basis of life. At the same time, with indomitable creative resilience, Sioux society, faced with the demise of important institutions as their warrior pursuits and the annual observance of the Sun Dance, filled the voids by originating new aspects of their own religious expression and social customs.

In the arts the period was one of intense experimental change and development. Not surprisingly, with the increased leisure at hand, the period also witnessed a tremendous surge of artistic production. Although the bison herds were depleted, government ration cattle provided some hides, and hunting of smaller game sporadically continued. Government annuities brought in still other materials, like blankets and woven fabrics. In the decorative arts, experimentation was rife as expert beadworkers and quill workers industriously decorated and embellished an unusual array of garments and other items. Indeed, no item to be considered for decoration seemed beyond their achievement.

Significantly, the period also witnessed the form of narrative painting striking its first roots in a new age.

SIOUX ARTISTS OF THE 20TH CENTURY

During the last quarter of the 19th century several technical changes in western Sioux narrative styles of painting had already developed. With the depletion of the bison herds, the increasing scarcity of hides and skins for painting prompted artists to more extensive experimentation with fabrics like muslin and canvas. Through contacts with military and agency personnel, paper was also made available and colored crayons, water colors and inks were introduced, replacing the use of powdered pigments.

While the vital tradition of narrative painting was cut off from its original source of motivation by the cessation of warrior pursuits, nevertheless several eventful developments ensued to provide continuity for the work of the creative Indian artist.

In fact, major innovative works on paper were created by Plains Indian artists during the last quarter of the 19th century and the first decades of the present century. During this time, several individuals who were profoundly and personally concerned by the vast changes which they witnessed taking place in the lives and customs of their tribe, spontaneously undertook production of complex pictorial documents recording the military, religious, and social histories and customs of their people. One of the most notable of these, Amos Bad Heart Bull, an Oglala Sioux from the Pine Ridge Reservation, worked from 1890 to 1913 on an impressive and monumental pictographic record of his people and their eventful history.

In addition to these inspired works, a new impetus for continued innovation in the narrative style, one with far-reaching implications for the future, resulted from the singular motivation of a developing new audience – the white man.

By the turn of the century a prodigious volume of work in the narrative style had been produced for white collectors – prompted in part by popular or scholarly curiosity of the Indian's unique subject matter, and at times out of a true admiration for his sheer inventiveness and versatility as an artist.

In the beginning, entire ledger books were often filled with page upon page of battle scenes and other exploits of warriors. Importantly, these commissioned works developed a greater variety of both subject and content, with manly exploits of warriors giving way to scenes of ceremonial performances, including visual reconstructions of the former Sun Dance rituals as well as scenes of the newly evolving ceremonial practices, like the "Grass Dance", which were then rapidly diffusing among the Plains tribes.

One of the most important Sioux artists of the period, whose work was continued well into the present century, was KILLS TWO, a Brule Sioux from the Rosebud Reservation in South Dakota. For some time Kills Two served as a tribal policeman on the Reservation, and he was highly regarded and respected in this capacity. He was also a versatile painter, working on both hides and muslin. Unlike the large and complex compositions of earlier narrative works executed on whole bison hides, Kills Two worked on a smaller scale, depicting only single subjects, somewhat in the spirit of easel painting.

Reflecting the growing diversification of subject matter in Sioux painting of the period, Kills Two's works include not only scenes of battle but also ceremonial performances, as well as dignified equestrian views of individuals dressed in their best finery (Catalogue 1).

By the turn of the century the Sioux had already ab-

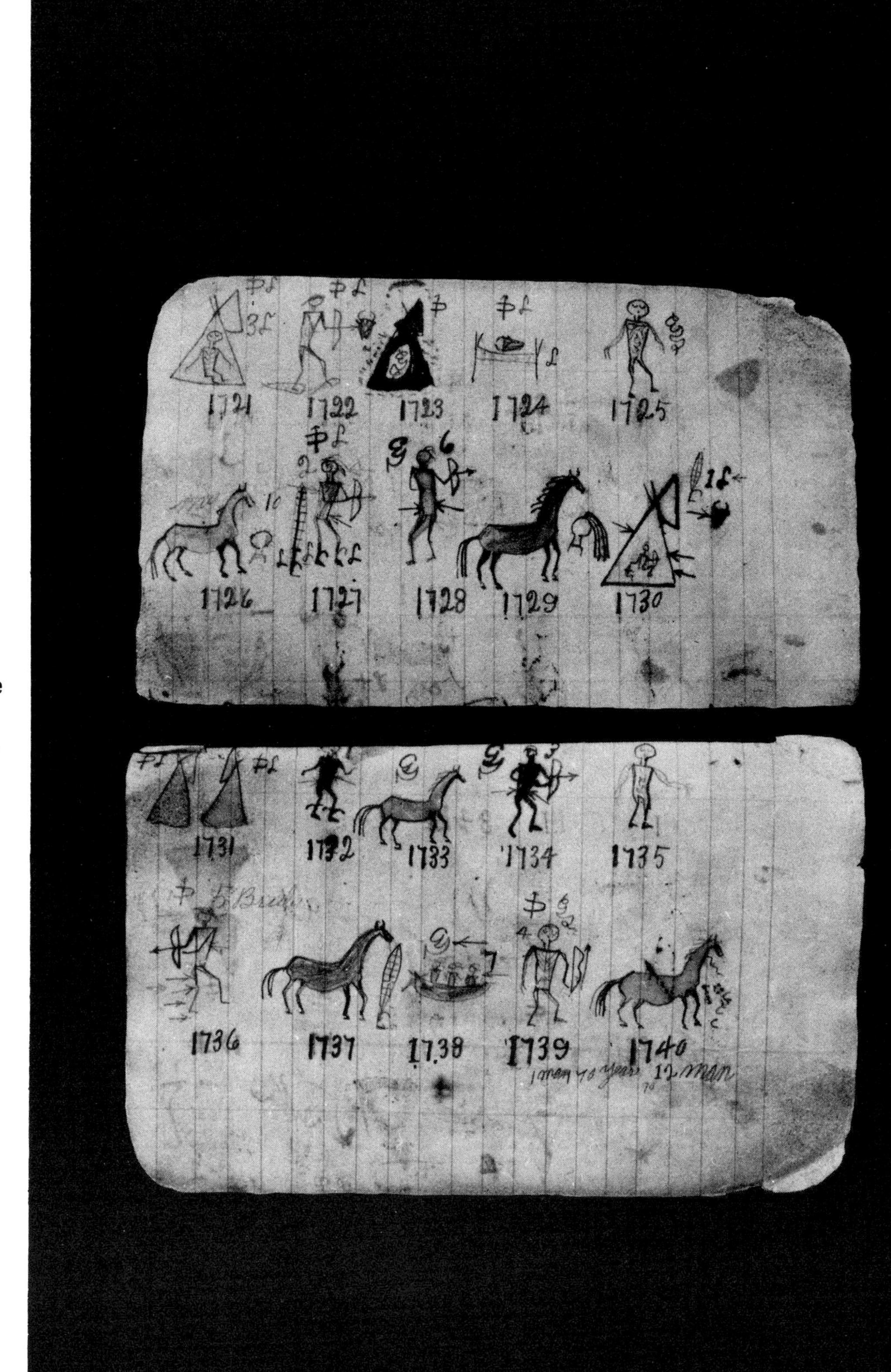

G Two pages from a WINTER COUNT, in book form, by Baptiste Good, a Brule Sioux. 19th to 20th centuries. Ink and watercolor on paper, each page 3½ x 6″. Gift of Mrs. Alice Brosius. (60.1)

sorbed the abrupt transition to sedentary life in the modern age, vocational education programs were begun, and individuals began taking up farming, carpentry and other trades within their respective reservation communities.

One of the most famed schools of the era was the Carlisle Indian School, located in Pennsylvania, a vocational education training facility which was attended by a number of Sioux youth of the period.

One individual who began his training at the Carlisle Indian School in 1911 was MOSES STRANGER HORSE, who, like the earlier artist, Kills Two, was a Brule from the Rosebud Reservation. During the First World War, Stranger Horse served in France where he remained for a brief period after the Armistice to pursue his interest in training and experience in the formal techniques and composition of oil painting.

Returning to the United States he toured throughout the west following the wild west show-rodeo circuit, gaining his income by public demonstrations of his artistry. Among his accomplishments was novel dexterity, performing feats such as painting with both hands, or working on upsidedown compositions, to the fascination and wonder of his audiences.

Stranger Horse was the first Sioux artist of the present century to make a definite break with both the stylistic conventions and war exploit subject matter of 19th century narrative painting. With all the progressive adventuresomeness inherent in the character of the western Sioux, Stranger Horse took the first bold step of any modern Sioux artist to intentionally and completely master what was still the foreign art forms of the white man.

Although he continued to depict scenes of 19th century Plains Indian life, he cast these subjects in fully painted landscape settings reminiscent of the paintings of grandiose scenery as popularized in the United States during the early 20th century.

His best works in fact are highly romanticized, sweeping vistas of western mountain ranges, containing incidental views of Sioux Indians in idyllic scenes of camping, on the trail (Catalogue 2), or action views of a mounted hunter bringing down a bison.

Stranger Horse, who signed his works "Sundown", was a unique phenomenon in that he not only gained a popular fame among white audiences in western states, but also was widely regarded among the Sioux of the Rosebud and Pine Ridge Reservations in South Dakota, where he inspired a following among other budding, self-taught artists, an influence which is in strong evidence to this day.

Another Brule artist from the Rosebud Reservation, GODFREY BROKEN ROPE, has followed in Stranger Horse's footsteps by also producing landscape paintings. Now living in Montana, Broken Rope's work is done in a muted palette of neutral tones, executed in simple house paints. His paintings are exclusively landscapes, seldom containing even a suggestion of a human figure. The majority of his compositions are devoted to nostalgic scenes reflecting life on the Rosebud Reservation, featuring views of early 20th century ranches with log cabins, often emphatically capturing the vast, silent beauty of the South Dakota plains (Catalogue 3).

Given the impetus of Stranger Horse's example, on the neighboring Pine Ridge Reservation oil painting has proliferated and a virtual colony of self-taught artists has sprung up. Among the first of the Pine Ridge painters was the Oglala Sioux, JAKE HERMAN, another individual who, like Stranger Horse, was a student of the early Carlisle Indian School. He continued to work in oils until his death in 1969. Unlike Stranger Horse however, Herman's paintings were obviously the product of an artist completely untutored and inexperienced in the techniques or subtleties of oil painting, but the best of his rugged and uncompromising compositions, despite their sentimental references, were sometimes powerful, highly personal, statements of the passing of the old way of life (Catalogue 4).

VINCENT BAD HEART BULL, another of the Pine Ridge artists, is a descendant of Amos Bad Heart Bull, whose important pictographic history of the Oglalas was mentioned earlier. Vincent's work, following in the tradition of the elder Bad Heart Bull, covers a variety of subjects documenting life and customs of the Oglala during the 19th century (Catalogue 5).

EDWARD TWO BULLS, also an Oglala from the Pine Ridge Reservation, paints a wide-ranging variety of subjects devoted to Indian life of the 19th century. However, his favored subjects are action-packed scenes of mounted Indians in the heat of an exciting and courageous bison hunt (Catalogue 6). The frankly anecdotal viewpoint of his works – stressing the manly vigor of a now passed rugged frontier life – is sympathetic with the type of western subject matter popularized and romanticized by the famed artists, Frederic Remington and Charles Russell.

In yet another vein, a unique and wholly original work in the medium of oil painting has been created by FRANK WHITE BUFFALO MAN, a Hunkpapa Sioux from the Cheyenne River Reservation in South Dakota, who is a grandson of the great Hunkpapa war chief and shaman, Sitting Bull. Although White Buffalo Man is also self-taught, his scenes of mounted warriors on the High Plains are presented within the visionary and romantic framework of an inspired artist. Indeed, his best

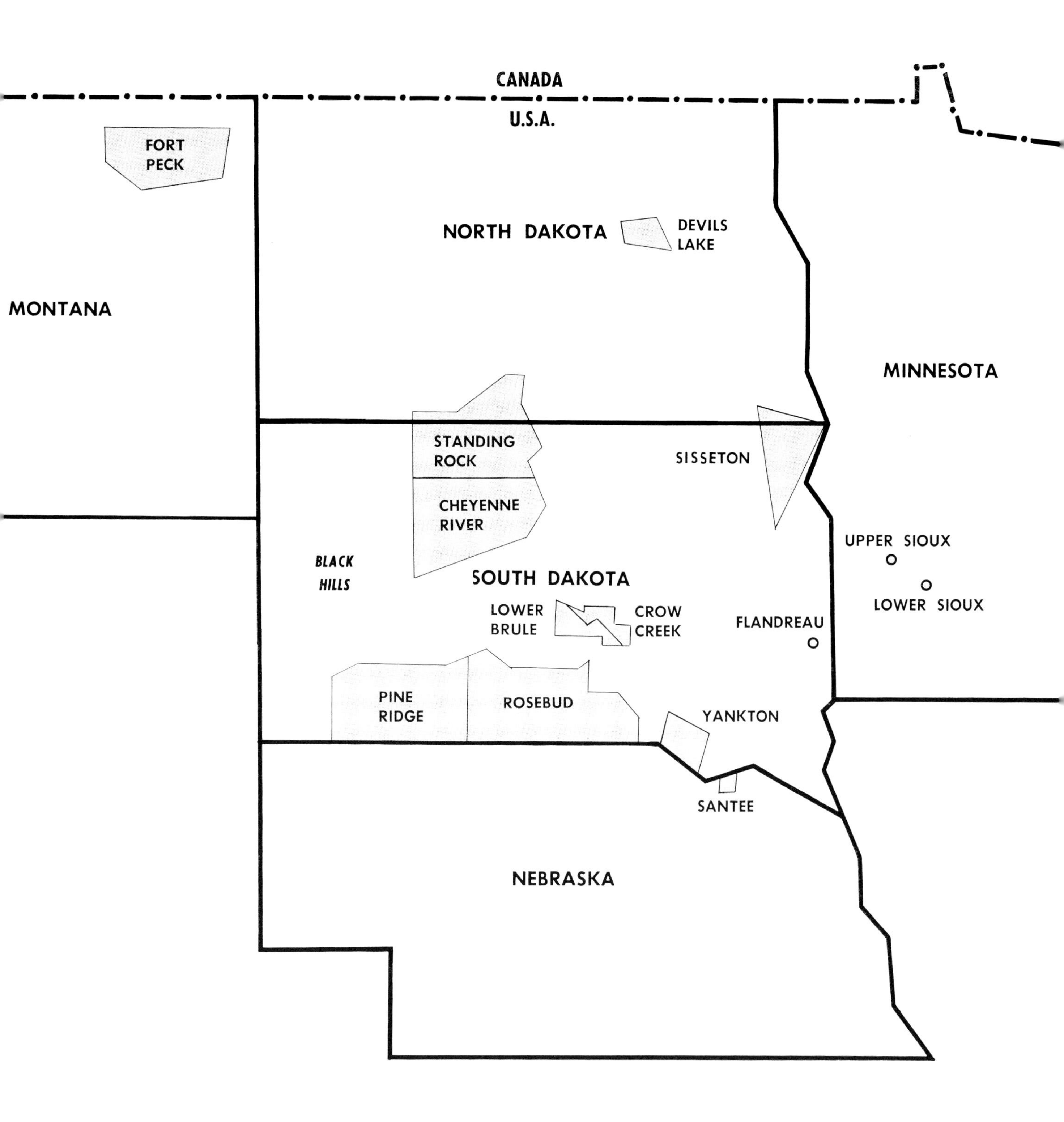

SIOUX RESERVATIONS

works are inventively crafted, highly individual compositions, executed with a brilliant and varied use of rich color (Catalogue 7).

While the singular attainment of western concepts of oil painting by Moses Stranger Horse helped give inspiration to innumerable self-taught Sioux artists who began work in oils, his example of gaining professional training and experience in fine arts also forecast important and fast-paced developments among forthcoming generations.

In 1929 the United States was shaken by a great economic depression, and in its wake a new era of the arts evolved. During the 1930s a variety of special programs were begun by the Federal Government to economically aid artists and the cultural community throughout the Nation. Under the spur of these massive Federal programs, artists in every part of the Nation were soon engaged in a variety of projects for contemporary artistic creations and productions, while universities, museums and other cultural institutions undertook work toward an avid research of all ramifications of the Nation's diverse cultural roots. Within a brief period virtually every aspect of artistic creativity in the United States was involved, including the contemporary arts of the American Indian.

As a result of these public programs American arts naturally developed a social consciousness, evolving strong regionalistic ideals. To be sure, the programs and developments of the period, as well as their results, were widely varied. Nevertheless, under their influence, the contemporary Indian artist, and his long and distinctive artistic heritage born of the North American soil, was soon effectively projected into the public consciousness of the entire Nation.

This remarkable era witnessed the emergence of a number of important contemporary artists of western Sioux descent, each of whom was variously influenced by their initial participation in one or more of the special programs or activities of the period. However, of the several major artists of Sioux descent who matured out of this period each, ultimately and characteristically, developed a marked individuality of style.

One of the important Federal art programs of the 1930s, administered by the United States Department of the Treasury, in which a number of Indian artists of the period participated, offered commissions for the creation of murals in public buildings. Private organizations and institutions soon followed suit, offering similar commissions. Within the decade, post offices, museums, churches and other public buildings in many western states were decorated by various contemporary Indian artists from the Plains and Southwest areas.

A Sioux artist whose career was first inspired by the mural activities of the period, who developed into one of the most noteworthy American painters of the era, was ANDREW STANDING SOLDIER, an Oglala born on the Pine Ridge Reservation of South Dakota. Educated in local schools of the Reservation area, Standing Soldier gained his first experience in the fine arts through mural commissions for the decoration of Bureau of Indian Affairs schools on the Pine Ridge Reservation in South Dakota and on the Standing Rock Reservation in North Dakota. However, after completing several other public commissions, including a Post Office in Valentine, Nebraska, Standing Soldier settled on the Pine Ridge Reservation where he began creation of smaller works, in the medium of watercolors. While he also painted imaginary views of 19th century life depicting the historic customs and pursuits of his people, his stature as an important American artist of the mid 20th century is nevertheless most clearly evident in his forthright interpretations of contemporary Sioux life. His later compositions in watercolors are, in fact, among his most distinguished works, devoted as they are to vivid but intimate views of Indian ranching and other activities, reflecting the distinctively western rural flavor of contemporary life on the Sioux reservations of South Dakota (Catalogue 8, 9, and 10).

With a delicate palette limited to greens, ochres and browns, and executed in a technique of deft, impressionistic brushwork, Standing Soldier's compositions are nevertheless strong and impressive by virtue of his masterful handling of form and space, a natural outgrowth of his early experience with monumental design as required by mural painting technique.

As one of the finest American regional artists of the period, Standing Soldier's watercolors deserve a much wider, national recognition than he received during his lifetime on the reservation. In addition, as the first contemporary artist of Sioux descent to produce forthright works interpreting an unromanticized and utterly honest view of contemporary life evolving on the Indian reservations of his home state, Standing Soldier's works are among the masterpieces of creative Sioux arts of the 20th century.

To be sure a number of contemporary Indian artists of the period were entering the mainstream of the Nation's artistic production, no longer to be regarded as the isolated spectacle of a Moses Stranger Horse.

Another important development of the period was the rise of a group movement in contemporary Indian art. Within the context of their direct participation in the public art programs and special education activities directed to Indian youth which were generated during the 1930s, contemporary Indian artists of various regions were, for the first time on an inter-tribal basis, consolidated in a surge of creativity which ultimately promulgated and promoted a distinctive national Indian school of illustrational painting.

As early as the 1920s, an experimental educational program was begun by the Art Department of the University of Oklahoma, which offered informal instruction in water-base media to encourage a number of Southern Plains Indian youth in an effort to evolve a distinctive, contemporary Indian art as an outgrowth of the 19th century narrative style of Plains Indian painting. This basic concept was further formalized in 1932 by the establishment of a small art department at the United States Indian School in Santa Fe, New Mexico, operated by the Bureau of Indian Affairs of the United States Department of the Interior. Known as The Studio, this educational program was directed to Indian youth of the numerous Southwestern tribes – the Pueblos, Navajo and Apache of the states of New Mexico and Arizona. In addition, several youths representative of the Plains Indian tribes of South Dakota and Oklahoma also attended. Students of this educational program undertook a consciously guided exploration of the historic tribal arts of the 19th century and were encouraged to adapt similar concepts to more modern, but equally stylized compositions, executed in tempera, casein, watercolor and other contemporary water-base media. As encouraged by these two educational programs, the illustrational works by students were directed to subjects either of imaginary, interpretative renderings of the customs and economic pursuits of the tribal past, or of contemporary scenes depicting figures in tribal dress participating in the ceremonial life of their respective tribal communities. For the most part these subjects were executed in crisply delineated figures placed against a sparce or unrelieved ground, much in the spirit of the 19th century narrative style of Plains Indian painting, which remained a major inspirational resource for this contemporary school of Indian art.

Although comparatively few youths from the northern Plains areas participated in these programs, nevertheless several individuals of Sioux descent, who have been directly or indirectly influenced by this pervasive movement, have developed into important artists.

A highly talented Sioux youth of the period whose career as an artist was encouraged by the various public programs of the period was CALVIN LARVIE, a Brule from the Rosebud Reservation. Larvie undertook his art training at Bacone College High School in Muskogee, Oklahoma, where he received instruction from Woodrow Wilson Crumbo, a Creek-Pottawatomie artist who himself had studied painting under the programs offered by the University of Oklahoma. Working in the highly formalized concepts of the stylized compositions in water-base media as encouraged by the training projects of the 1920s and 30s, Larvie developed a sensitive draftsmanship which he applied to decorative works of considerable charm (Catalogue 11). In 1939, Larvie was commissioned by the Indian Arts and Crafts Board of the United States Department of the Interior to execute a large mural decoration depicting mounted Plains Indian hunters, which was featured in an extensive exhibition of historic and contemporary tribal arts of the United States that the Board organized for presentation in the United States Federal Pavilion at the Golden Gate International Exposition in San Francisco. Tragically, Larvie's promising career was cut short as he was seriously disabled during World War II and, regrettably, produced little work after 1940.

OSCAR HOWE, a Yanktonai born on the Crow-Creek Reservation in South Dakota, began his early training at The Studio of the Santa Fe Indian School in New Mexico. One of the few Plains Indian youth attending The Studio, Howe went on to gain degrees in art education at the Dakota Wesleyan University and at the University of Oklahoma. While Howe's early work is obviously a product of the stylized and simplified representational painting promulgated by The Studio, his later work is individualistic and highly experimental. After military service during World War II, Howe returned to take up a series of paintings done in a monochromatic range of warm earth tones (Catalogue 12). However, during the 1950s as the arts of the United States witnessed an international ascendance, Howe abandoned the purely illustrational objectives of his earlier works and turned to a more vital, contemporary concept. He began experimentation with cubism, ultimately developing a rich palette of bold color, masterfully stated in increasingly complex compositions (Catalogue 13 and 14).

A frequent exhibitor and prize-winner at national Indian art exhibitions in western states, Howe has gained a formidable national and international reputation as one of the outstanding artists of Indian descent today. Howe has also become one of the most respected art educators, now Professor of Art at the Art Department of the University of South Dakota in Vermillion. Through the example of his own achievement as a creative artist, as well as by his activities as a professional educator, Howe has encouraged and directed the development of a number of other important contemporary Sioux artists, several of whom are represented in this exhibition.

One such individual is HERMAN RED ELK, a Yanktonai born on the Fort Peck Reservation in Montana, who began his career as an electrician. Red Elk first became interested in art as a result of occupational training during a period of hospitalization at the Sioux Sanitorium in Rapid City, South Dakota. After his recuperation he participated in short term art training programs at the Black Hills State College in Spearfish, South Dakota, and for two successive summers in Indian culture workshops, directed by Oscar Howe, at the University of South Dakota. Red Elk's best works to date are stylized representations done in casein on illustration board, depicting subjects ranging from mounted warriors to ceremonial dances (Catalogue 15 and 16). An excellent draftsman and illustrator, Red Elk continues to experiment in a diversity of media and techniques (Catalogue 17). During 1962 he undertook a project sponsored by the Indian Arts and Crafts Board's Sioux Indian Museum and Crafts Center in Rapid City to reconstruct a series of painted bison hides, executed with aboriginal-style bone implements and powdered pigments, with compositions in both the geometric and narrative forms of 19th century Sioux hide painting.

One of the most individualistic artists of Sioux descent today, and one of the first to make a total break with 19th century aboriginal subject matter, is TOM CLAYMORE, a Sans Arc born on the Cheyenne River Reservation of South Dakota. After a brief period of art instruction during his early education at Haskell Institute in Kansas, Claymore went on to receive further education in other fields at a variety of colleges and universities throughout the country. Concentrating on the exploration of contemporary styles and media, during the past two decades Claymore has taken up the production of a wide diversity of unique works, with ingenious and imaginative interpretations of subjects ranging from historic western Americana (Catalogue 18) to vividly contemporary subjects, executed in an intentionally naieve style. With a masterful handling of composition and technique, Claymore's works reveal a playfully sophisticated and sometimes sardonic humor, a characteristic often evident in even the best of his more experimental paintings (Catalogue 19 and 20).

The experimental work by the outstanding personalities to emerge during the 1940s and 50s has been avidly embraced by a new generation of artists of Sioux descent who often project their work within the varied framework of the most popular or avant-garde styles of painting current on the national scene in the United States. Similar to artists of any national origin in the United States, individuals of the younger generation of Sioux artists are gravitating to urban centers or obtaining teaching positions at campuses of the larger educational institutions in western states. The present period vividly reflects the thrust of Indian society into the variety of contemporary experiences in the United States, contrasting sharply with the isolationism of reservation life during the first quarter of the 20th century.

One of the younger generation artists of the post World War II period is CHARLES TRIMBLE, an Oglala Sioux born on the Pine Ridge Reservation. Although Trimble is currently gaining a professional education in journalism, he has continued an early interest in fine arts, working primarily in oils. Now living in Boulder, Colorado, where he attends school, during the past several years Trimble has executed experimental works in cubism, directed to subjects of contemporary Plains Indian dancers (Catalogue 21).

ROBERT FREEMEN, of part Yanktonai Sioux and part San Louisano descent, was born in Rincon, California. Like Trimble, Freeman's work is devoted to subject matter interpreting the varied aspects of contemporary Indian life. An excellent draftsman, Freeman produces powerful images in both oil and ink sketches (Catalogue 22).

One of the younger generation artists of Sioux descent who has gained a professional education in the arts is ARTHUR AMIOTTE, an Oglala Sioux born on the Pine Ridge Reservation. During a brief early period, Amiotte's first works were executed in water-base media on illustration board, devoted to subjects of 19th century Indian culture, stylistically executed in the vein of Oscar Howe's later works. However, during the past five years Amiotte has diversified his own work tremendously, experimenting widely in abstract paintings of free and vigorous brushwork, with rich textural surfaces. He has also experimented in fine craft media and has already completed an impressive series of colorful abstract wall hangings in applique and stitchery techniques, as well as three-dimensional constructions of woven and netted forms. As a result of the past years of experimentation and mastery of new forms, Amiotte's painting today has gained a mature and expressive imagery distinctively his own (Catalogue 23). His most recent works are often directed to interpretations of western landscape which are at once lyrical and symbolic, expressive of the forces and mysteries of the High Plains homelands of his people (Catalogue 24 and 25).

As a graduate of Northern State College in South Dakota, and of the Pennsylvania State University, Amiotte is also a professional educator. After several years of teaching art education at Northern State College, Amiotte has returned to his home reservation, where he is now devoting his abilities to teaching at the Porcupine Day School.

The latest and one of the most prodigious talents to emerge among the younger generation of Sioux artists is ROBERT PENN, born in Omaha, Nebraska, of part Sioux and part Omaha descent. Penn is currently studying art under Oscar Howe at the University of South Dakota where he has already produced an impressive number of bold, forceful abstractions. Penn's work fairly vibrates with a lively energy, expressed through abstract compositions of organic forms which sweep across the canvas, executed with a vivid, plastic use of pigment and rich color. His larger paintings already approach the grand scale of today's best monumental works, devoted as they often are to a universal content, holding a promise which only the future can reveal (Catalogue 26). He has also produced a number of works with distinctively Indian themes, projecting old subjects into a poetic, modern idiom (Catalogue 27 and 28).

The training and development of contemporary artists of Sioux descent have recently found renewed impetus through a special educational program established on the site of the earlier Santa Fe Indian School. Known as the Institute of American Indian Arts, this program, operated by the Bureau of Indian Affairs of the United States Department of the Interior, is directed to contemporary Indian, Eskimo and Aleut youth from throughout the United States. Founded in 1962, the Institute offers a heritage-centered approach to self-development, stressing cultural roots as a basis for creative, individual expression. A wide range of media is offered, encompassing training in virtually every field of the arts – painting, graphics, sculpture, ceramics, textiles, exhibition arts, photography, as well as drama, music, the dance, creative writing and a limited offering in commercial art.

A number of contemporary Sioux youth attending the Institute have already developed a diversity of personal statements which forecast the many directions in which painting created by artists of Sioux descent may ultimately branch.

EARL EDER, a Yanktonai from the Fort Peck Reservation of Montana, was one of the earlier Sioux students at the Institute. Eder's work is devoted to large-scale paintings of massive images focusing on objects drawn from the Sioux cultural past, like pipe bags or shields, executed with a dynamic and forceful handling of pigment (Catalogue 29). Eder is currently attending the San Francisco Art Institute where he is working toward a degree in fine arts.

AUSTIN RAVE, another early Institute student, is a Miniconjou Sioux from the Cheyenne River Reservation in South Dakota. One of the several Institute students whose work is often devoted to statements with social implications, Rave's large canvases loom with overpowering, sometimes brooding, images of historical import (Catalogue 30).

By contrast, DUANE LAFFERTY, an Oglala from the Pine Ridge Reservation, directs his work to understated but effective compositions, sometimes drawing upon the most venerable themes from the ancient tribal past (Catalogue 31).

DON MONTILEAUX, also an Oglala from the Pine Ridge Reservation, has begun work on a series of brilliant hard edge abstractions, inspired in part by the geometric arts of 19th century Sioux hide painting (Catalogue 32).

As one of the most articulate and astute spokesmen of the younger generation of Sioux artists, Arthur Amiotte has eloquently stated the case for the avid experimentation which has characterized recent painting by Sioux artists:

"The lifestyle of the American Indian today is no longer one of isolation and retreat into a static world of solid tradition. He is affected by the forces of technology in its myriad forms and has indeed submitted to the seductive overtures of rapid social change that an electrified world produces.

"As a result, the stabilizing force that once gave rise to a native art indigenous to a particular group has been diminished to a degree that no longer can one say, with good conscience, that a particular art form is purely representative or indigenous to a particular group. Nor can one say any longer that a particular person belonging to a distinct group of Indians should only produce certain kinds of art forms.

"Recognizing this, one should indeed extend the same privileges and freedom of thought, experimentation, and discovery to native artists, in the sense that they too are participants and citizens in an ever changing world culture, wrought and typified by experimentation and discovery.

"This is not to say every native artist should subscribe wholeheartedly to every avant-garde movement in the arts and dump any reference to his cultural heritage. This is a psychological impossibility.

"By his very being, the native artist has deep roots in a type of cultural thinking, whether he is aware of it on a conscious level or not, which can provide him with a unique source, a well-spring for imbuing his works with a particular flavor that directly or indirectly spells American Indian. Such an approach extends and presents to the modern world in which he lives, subtleties about

the American Indian today. Presented are the numerous effects on his psyche, be they negative or positive, of the modern world."

The twenty artists represented in this exhibition were chosen to illustrate the diverse avenues of self-expression which have been taken by artists of Sioux descent during the 20th century, from the early generations of self-taught artists to those of the youthful student artist experimenting with the latest avant-garde styles of painting advocated by the Nation's cultural centers. In particular, the works in this exhibition were selected and organized to present the course of development, from the first spontaneous exploration of new media, to the increasing pursuit of varied educational experiences, which are projecting Sioux painting today into the challenging realm of professional fine arts in the United States.

If one may judge future developments from past achievement, few can doubt that during the present century American artists of Sioux descent, whose work so often in the past has been characterized by striking individuality, will benefit by the stimuli of increased experimentation and diversification, and from their native genius deeply rooted in the inspiring and enduring environment of the High Plains, will continue to develop creative and valid artistic statements, distinctively and undeniably their own.

Myles Libhart
Director of Museums, Exhibitions
and Publications

PHOTOGRAPH CREDITS

All photographs are from the files of the Indian Arts and Crafts Board of the U.S. Department of the Interior, with the following exceptions: Jake Kills In Sight, *illus. p. 28;* Nancy Whitehorse, *illus. p. 30;* University of South Dakota, *illus. p. 48;* Charles Trimble, *illus. p. 60;* Robert Freeman, *illus. p. 62;* Institute of American Indian Arts, *illus. p. 72;* Austin Rave, *illus. p. 74;* Duane Lafferty, *illus. p. 76.*

THE ARTISTS AND THEIR WORKS

Illustrations of the artist's works have been arranged to suggest the course of development of Sioux painting during the 20th century, to reflect the increasing professionalism and experimentation of the past several decades.

The date following each title is that inscribed on the work of art by the artist; otherwise the date is enclosed in parenthesis.

All dimensions are in inches; height precedes width.

All works of art are from the Indian art collections of the Indian Arts and Crafts Board; catalogue numbers for the works of art are given in parenthesis at the end of each caption.

KILLS TWO

Tribal band: Brule. Born on the northeastern High Plains, 1859 – died Mellette County, South Dakota, on the Rosebud Reservation, 1927. Served as a Tribal Policeman on the Rosebud Reservation, and as an Indian Scout for the U.S. Army during the Ghost Dance Uprising, (1890-91). Produced numerous paintings on hide and muslin; subjects included warrior pursuits, ceremonial dances, individuals on horseback, reconstructions of calendrical histories.

1 KILLS TWO: *Sioux Man on a Horse.* 1889. Watercolor, ink and crayon on muslin, 9 3/8 x 8 3/8". John A. Anderson Collection (620)

MOSES STRANGER HORSE

Tribal band: Brule. Born near Wood, South Dakota, on the Rosebud Reservation, 1890 – died Rosebud Reservation, South Dakota, 1941. Entered Carlisle Indian School, Pennsylvania, 1911; served in U.S. Army during World War I , stationed in Paris where he remained after the Armistice to study oil painting. Traveled extensively throughout western United States appearing at rodeos and fairs, including New York World's Fair, 1939, giving public demonstrations of his technical dexterity as an artist; signed works by pseudonym, *Sundown.*

2 STRANGER HORSE: *On the Trail.* 1933. Oil on masonite, 23½ x 47". John A. Anderson Collection (979)

GODFREY BROKEN ROPE

TOHANNI KU SNI: Never Returns. Tribal band: Brule. Born Okreek, South Dakota, on the Rosebud Indian Reservation, 1908. Attended Rapid City Indian School, South Dakota; graduated Flandreau Indian School, South Dakota, 1928. Since 1950 has traveled extensively throughout western United States as self-made minister of the gospel, also presents public demonstrations of his self-taught style of painting. Lives in Billings, Montana.

"You give something to Christ in place of what you get. You give Christ your sin habit, and he gives you eternal life in its place. It's like taking things off store shelves. You can't have them until you pay for them. I do not talk white man lingo unless you want to buy a picture. But if you talk about Jesus Christ I will stop my painting and visit with you."

– Godfrey Broken Rope

3 BROKEN ROPE: *Indian Ranch on the Rosebud.* (1969). House paint on masonite, 12 x 31¾". (W-69.2.11)

JAKE HERMAN

IGLA-KA TERILA: Loves To Move Camp. Tribal band: Oglala. Born Pine Ridge Agency, South Dakota, 1892 – died Rapid City, South Dakota, 1969. Attended Rapid City Indian School, South Dakota, 1903-06, 1907-10; Holy Rosary Mission, South Dakota, 1907; Carlisle Indian School, Pennsylvania, 1914-16. Performed as a clown with various wild west show-rodeos, including the Rodeo Royal Circus and Jack King's Wild West Show. Served as a tribal council member of the Oglala Sioux Tribe on Pine Ridge Reservation, South Dakota, for 19 years and was on the Tribal Executive Board for 6 years. During later years settled at Kyle, South Dakota, on the Pine Ridge Reservation, where, as a self-taught artist, he produced oil paintings; wrote column, WA HO SI, in *THE SHANNON COUNTY NEWS*, Pine Ridge, South Dakota; also wrote Oglala legends, folktales and historic sketches, as well as autobiographical articles, which he illustrated and published by ditto and mimeograph.

"Many moons ago, long before 'civilized man' invaded the Happy Hunting Grounds of the Sioux Indians, legends and folklore were passed by word of mouth from generation to generation. The system of keeping track of years was by the winter counts. The month of the year was by moon, as in the 'moon of the cracking of the woods', meaning January . . . Pictures were drawn on buckskin telling of human events. I paint and write about, know and understand, these old time warriors who were untouched by formal education, schooled only by the elements of Mother Nature, a group of people who lived only on what Mother Nature offered them. From the echoes of dying embers of their campfires, from the time I was a small boy, down deep in my heart my thoughts were always of painting and writing about their legends, history, and folklore".

– *Jake Herman*

4 HERMAN: *End of the Trail.* (1967) Oil on masonite, 20½ x 22". Gift of Blackpipe State Bank, Martin, S.D. (67.1.1)

VINCENT BAD HEART BULL

HOSHILA WASTE: Good Boy. Tribal band: Oglala. Born Oglala, South Dakota, on the Pine Ridge Reservation, 1926. Attended Oglala Community School, 1939-47. A self-taught artist, began working in oils about 1959. Lives in Pine Ridge, South Dakota, on the Pine Ridge Reservation.

"I am fortunate I have acquired this media. I have learned a lot about my people, the culture which has enabled me to take up the challenge in this wonderful and interesting field."
— Vincent Bad Heart Bull.

5 BAD HEART BULL: *Moving Camp.* 1968. Oil on masonite, 16 x 24". (68.30.84)

EDWARD TWO BULL

HINHAN WICAHCA: Old Owl. Tribal band: Oglala. Born Pine Ridge, South Dakota, on the Pine Ridge Reservation, 1938. Attended Seventh Day Adventist Mission School, Red Shirt, South Dakota, and the Oglala Community School, both on the Pine Ridge Reservation. Owns and operates a horse ranch near Hermosa, South Dakota. A self-taught artist, works in oils. Lives in Hermosa, South Dakota.

"Painting to me at first was a challenge but has now become a way of life for me. Is there a better way of preserving the history and folklore of the old time Indians?"

– Edward Two Bulls.

6 TWO BULLS: *The Attack.* 1969. Oil on canvas panel, 18 x 24". (69.9.52)

FRANK WHITE BUFFALO MAN

Tribal band: Hunkpapa. A grandson of Sitting Bull, the famed Hunkpapa war chief and shaman. Born LaPlante, South Dakota, on the Cheyenne River Reservation, 1903. Attended Salem Indian School, Chemawa, Oregon; studied drama and commercial art at Black Hills State College, Spearfish, South Dakota. A champion butterfly dancer and rope spinner, during youth performed in Buffalo Bill's Wild West Circus, later toured with 101 Ranch Wild West Show, performed in Duhamel Sitting Bull Swing Pageant, Rapid City, South Dakota, appeared in moving pictures, and, most recently, several seasons with Crazy Horse Pageant, Hot Springs, South Dakota. A self-taught artist working in oils, has also given public demonstrations of his workmanship. Lives in Seattle, Washington.

"I hope someday to have my paintings in the Smithsonian like my grandfather has."

– *Frank White Buffalo Man*

7 WHITE BUFFALO MAN: *Two Scouts.* 1968. Oil on masonite, 21 x 24". (68.30.86)

ANDREW STANDING SOLDIER

Tribal band: Oglala. Born, Pine Ridge Reservation, 1917 – died Omaha, Nebraska, 1967. Attended Pine Ridge Boarding School and Oglala Community High School, both on Pine Ridge Reservation; encouraged to experiment with mural painting by special summer school art teachers at Oglala Community High School, summer 1937. Won fourth prize in poster design contest sponsored by Indian Arts and Crafts Board, U.S. Department of the Interior, for U.S. Federal Pavilion at Golden Gate International Exposition, San Francisco, California, 1939; received mural commissions U.S. Post Office, Blackfoot, Idaho, on the Fort Hall Reservation, 1939, Bureau of Indian Affairs school on Pine Ridge Reservation, South Dakota, 1940-41, and Standing Rock Reservation, North Dakota, 1940s, and U.S. Post Office, Valentine, Nebraska, 1940s. Settled on Pine Ridge Reservation during 1940s, began production of watercolors.

8 STANDING SOLDIER: *Branding Calves.* 1952. Watercolor on illustration board, 16½ x 22½". (70.2.2)

9 STANDING SOLDIER: *Indian Family Preparing Pemmican.* 1952. Watercolor on illustration board, 16½ x 22½". (70.2.6)

10 STANDING SOLDIER: *The Bronc Rider.* 1952. Watercolor on illustration board, 16½ x 22½".
(70.2.1)

CALVIN LARVIE

HEHAKA HANSKA: Tall Elk. Tribal band: Brule. Born Wood, South Dakota, on the Rosebud Reservation, 1920 – died Rapid City, South Dakota, 1969. Attended Rosebud Boarding School, near Mission, South Dakota, on the Rosebud Reservation, 1930s; studied painting under Woodrow Wilson Crumbo, Creek-Pottawattomi artist, at Bacone College High School, Muskogee, Oklahoma, graduated 1940. Mural commission from Indian Arts and Crafts Board, U.S. Department of the Interior, for U.S. Federal Pavilion at Golden Gate International Exposition, San Francisco, 1939. Disabled while serving in U.S. Army during World War II.

11 LARVIE: *The Buffalo Headdress.* ca. 1940. Casein on illustration board, 12¾ x 15". (69.23.25)

OSCAR HOWE

MAZUHA HOKSHINA: Trader Boy. Tribal band: Yanktonai. Born Joe Creek, South Dakota, on Crow Creek Reservation, 1915. Attended Pierre Indian School, South Dakota, 1933; studied painting at U.S. Indian School, Santa Fe, New Mexico, 1934-38; studied mural techniques at Indian Art Center, Fort Sill, Oklahoma, 1940; majored in fine arts at Dakota Wesleyan University, Mitchell, South Dakota, 1948-52 (B.A. degree); University of Oklahoma, Norman, Oklahoma, 1952-54 (M.F.A. degree). Art instructor at Pierre High School, South Dakota, 1939, and 1953-57; Artist in Residence and assistant instructor at Dakota Wesleyan University, 1948-52; Professor of Fine Arts and Artist in Residence, University of South Dakota, Vermillion, 1957 to present. Exhibited widely in group showings and one-man exhibitions; numerous awards and honors, including honorific title Artist Laureate of South Dakota conferred by Governor Herseth, 1960; named Fellow, International Institute of Art and Letters, Geneva, Switzerland, 1960; awarded a Certificate of Appreciation by Indian Arts and Crafts Board, U.S. Department of the Interior, 1962; awarded Waite Phillips Trophy for Outstanding Contributions to American Indian Art by Philbrook Art Center, Tulsa, Oklahoma, 1966. Commissions for murals include Civic Auditorium, Mobridge, South Dakota, 1942; has designed annual decorations for "World's Only Corn Palace", Mitchell, South Dakota, since 1948; designed ceramic tile mural for Proviso High School, Hinsdale, Illinois, 1956. Lives in Vermillion, South Dakota.

"One criterion for my painting is to present the cultural life and activities of the Sioux Indians; dances, ceremonies, legends, lore, arts . . . It is my greatest hope that my paintings may serve to bring the best things of Indian culture into the modern way of life."

— Oscar Howe

12 HOWE: *The Sioux Painter.* (1950). Casein on paper, 17 x 11". (65.22.10)

13 HOWE: *Dakota Eagle Dancer.* (1962). Casein on illustration board, 24¼ x 19½". (W-62.9)

14 HOWE: *Medicine Man.* (1962) Casein on illustration board, 20½ x 22½". (69.17.1)

HERMAN RED ELK

HEGAKA WAMBDI: Eagle Elk. Tribal band: Yanktonai. Born Poplar, Montana, on the Fort Peck Reservation, 1918. Attended Public School, Poplar, Montana; Salem Indian School, Chemawa, Oregon, 1935-39; studied drawing as occupational therapy at Sioux Sanitorium, Rapid City, South Dakota 1961-62; studied oil painting in workshop presented by Diane Tollefson at Black Hills State College, Spearfish, South Dakota, summer 1963; attended workshop in Contemporary Indian Art presented by Oscar Howe at University of South Dakota, Vermillion, summers 1964 and 1965. Undertook special projects at Indian Arts and Crafts Board's Sioux Indian Museum and Crafts Center in Rapid City, South Dakota, to reconstruct forms of 19th century hide painting utilizing aboriginal-style bone painting implements and powdered pigments, 1962. Executed commercial art designs for Great Western Enterprise, Rapid City, South Dakota, 1967-68; Museum Aid at the Sioux Indian Museum and Crafts Center, Rapid City, South Dakota, 1969 to present. Has exhibited widely in Indian art exhibits in Oklahoma, Arizona, Washington, D.C., and throughout South Dakota; demonstrated hide painting at Black Hills Exposition, Rapid City, South Dakota, 1965 and 1966. Lives in Rapid City, South Dakota.

"I enjoy painting; trying to recapture and preserve the very early traditions and life of our Sioux of the plains, their religion, their ceremonies, and their many ways of expressing themselves in their various art media."

— Herman Red Elk.

15 RED ELK: *Dakota Scout.* 1969. Acrylic on watercolor paper, 10 x 12". (69.8.1)

16 RED ELK: *Horse Dance.* 1969. Acrylic on watercolor paper 21 x 16½". (69.8.2)

17 RED ELK: *Attack.* 1970. Acrylic on canvas, 39¾ x 40¾". (70.3.1)

THOMAS CLAYMORE

NAPE SICA HOKSILA: Bad Hand Boy. Tribal band: Sans Arc. Born Cheyenne Agency, on the Cheyenne River Reservation, South Dakota, 1909. Attended Grammar School in LaPlante, South Dakota, on the Cheyenne River Reservation; Haskell Institute, Lawrence, Kansas, 1927-30, included art studies under Bill "Lone Star" Dietz; majored in history at Bacone Junior College, 1936-38; majored in biology at Redlands University, California, 1949-51; majored in psychology at Northern State College, Aberdeen, South Dakota, 1963; majored in counciling and guidance at University of North Dakota, Grand Forks, 1965 (B.F.A. degree); studied art at University of California, Los Angeles, 1966. Resumed painting during early 1960s, began experiments with acrylics, has exhibited widely throughout the United States. Lives in Chadron, Nebraska.

"Though I am an Indian I have studiously avoided traditional Indian art partly because of a lack of knowledge of the lore, but mostly to keep myself in a "reach out" experimental position to evolve a modern style. Over the past year and a half, I have worked out the media which I will hence employ. I consider myself a "now man" – a colorist with expertise in this media, I will subtly include the Indianess of me in my work I know."

– Tom Claymore.

18 CLAYMORE: *The Dry Spell.* 1964. Oil and acrylic on illustration board, 27 9/16 x 39 5/8".
(W-66.55.2)

19 CLAYMORE: *Cause II.* (1965). Acrylic on watercolor paper, 20¼ x 14 15/16". Gift of the Artist. (W-66.44)

20 CLAYMORE: *Les Girls.* (1965). Oil on masonite, 17 5/8 x 18 7/16". (W-66.55.1)

CHARLES TRIMBLE

CHUN SHA SHA: Red Willow. Tribal band: Oglala. Born Wanblee, South Dakota, on the Pine Ridge Reservation, 1935. Attended Holy Rosary Mission, Pine Ridge, South Dakota, 1940-52; studied industrial arts at Cameron State Agricultural College, Lawton, Oklahoma, 1952-54; studied fine arts at University of South Dakota, Vermillion, 1954-57; studying journalism at University of Colorado, Boulder, 1968 to present. Illustrator for Mark Greenwalt Advertising, Spokane, Washington, 1960; master schedules analyst for General Dynamics/Astronautics, 1961-64. Has exhibited in Indian art exhibitions in western states, including Indian Art Exhibit in LaGrande, Oregon, 1960, and art exhibit at the All American Indian Days in Sheridan, Wyoming, 1963 and 1966, for which he won prizes. Lives in Boulder, Colorado.

21 TRIMBLE: *Dancer.* 1967. Oil on canvas, 24 1/8 x 18 1/8". (69.15.3)

ROBERT FREEMAN

Tribal band: Yanktonai; (mother, Yanktonai Sioux from Crow Creek Reservation, South Dakota; father, San Louisano from Rincon Reservation, California). Born Valley Center, California, on Rincon Reservation, 1939. Graduated public schools in Escondido, California, 1957; attended Mira Costa Junior College, Oceanside, California. Began painting in 1961; also works in pen and ink drawing, welded metal sculptures and wood carving. Works exhibited widely throughout the United States. Lives in San Marcos, California.

"I consider myself in the learning process and desire to express my impressions of our American way of life."
– Robert Freeman.

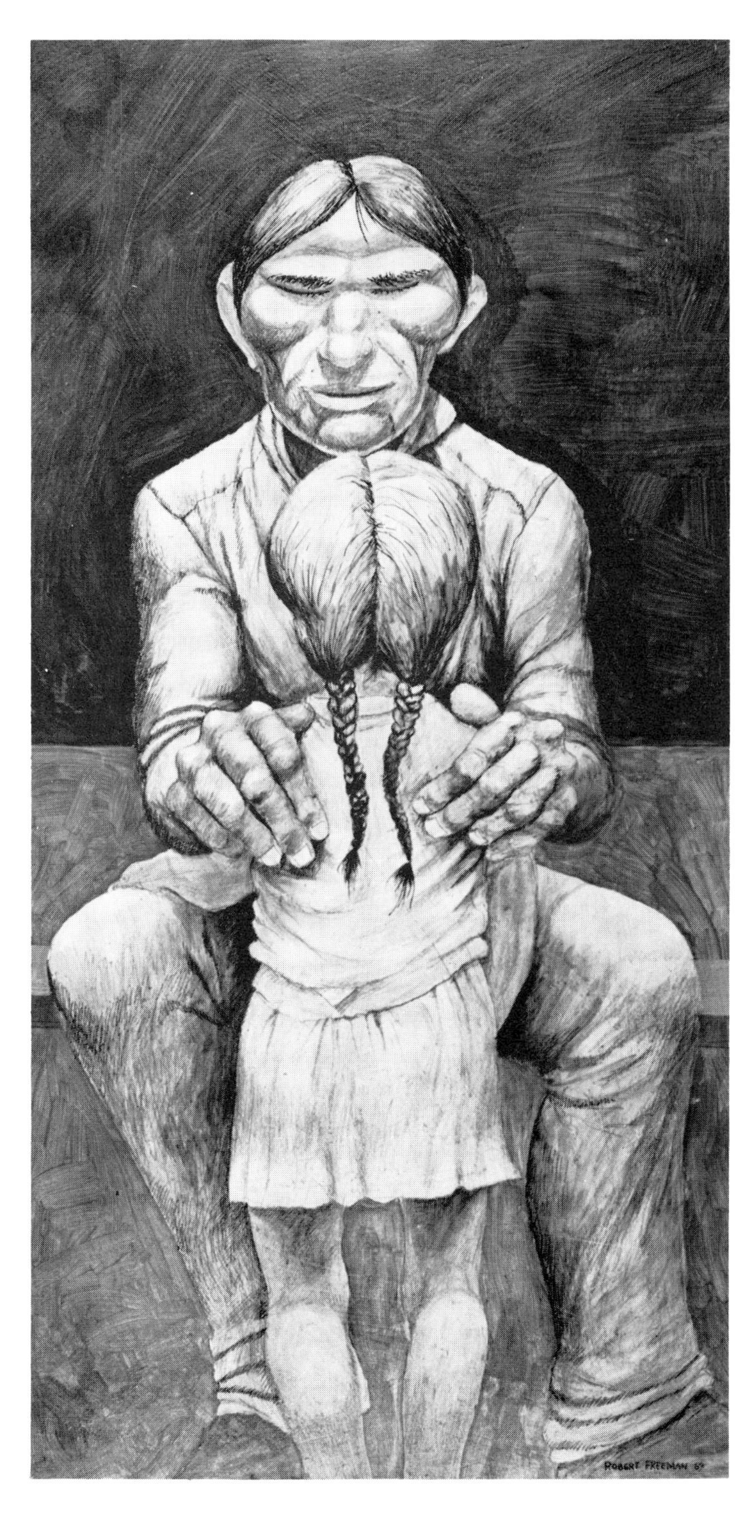

22 FREEMAN: *This Is All That Matters.*
1969. Acrylic and India ink on masonite,
24 x 11 7/8". (69.19.1)

ARTHUR AMIOTTE

WARPA TANKA KUCIYELA: Low Black Bird. Tribal band: Oglala. Born Pine Ridge, South Dakota, on the Pine Ridge Reservation, 1942. Attended public schools in Custer, South Dakota, 1948-60; workshop in Contemporary Indian Art presented by Oscar Howe at University of South Dakota, Vermillion, summer 1961; studied art education at Northern State College, Aberdeen, South Dakota 1960-64 (B.S. degree); Oklahoma University, Norman, 1966; Pennsylvania State University, University Park, 1967-69 (M.S. degree). Art instructor at Woodrow Wilson Jr. High School, Sioux City, Iowa, 1964-66; instructor of art and art education at Northern State College, Aberdeen, South Dakota, 1966-69; instructor at Porcupine Day School, Porcupine, South Dakota, on the Pine Ridge Reservation, 1969 to present. Works exhibited widely in group shows and one-man exhibitions in South Dakota and throughout the United States; awarded numerous prizes and honors, including Merit Award, Annual Fall Exhibition, Sioux City Art Center, Iowa, 1965, First Place Grand Award, Foundation of North American Indian Culture Exhibition, 1964. Lives in Porcupine, South Dakota.

"Being an Indian, I believe from the time I was very young I was taught by my grandparents who reared me to be sensitive to things as well as to sounds and colors . . . growing up with this sensitivity you eventually learn to see and hear only as an Indian."

– Arthur Amiotte.

23 AMIOTTE: *Life Cells.* 1969. Casein and fabric collage on masonite, 30 x 23 7/8". (69.22.4)

24 AMIOTTE: *Land Formations.* (1969). Casein and fabric collage on masonite, 23 7/8 x 30". (69.22.3)

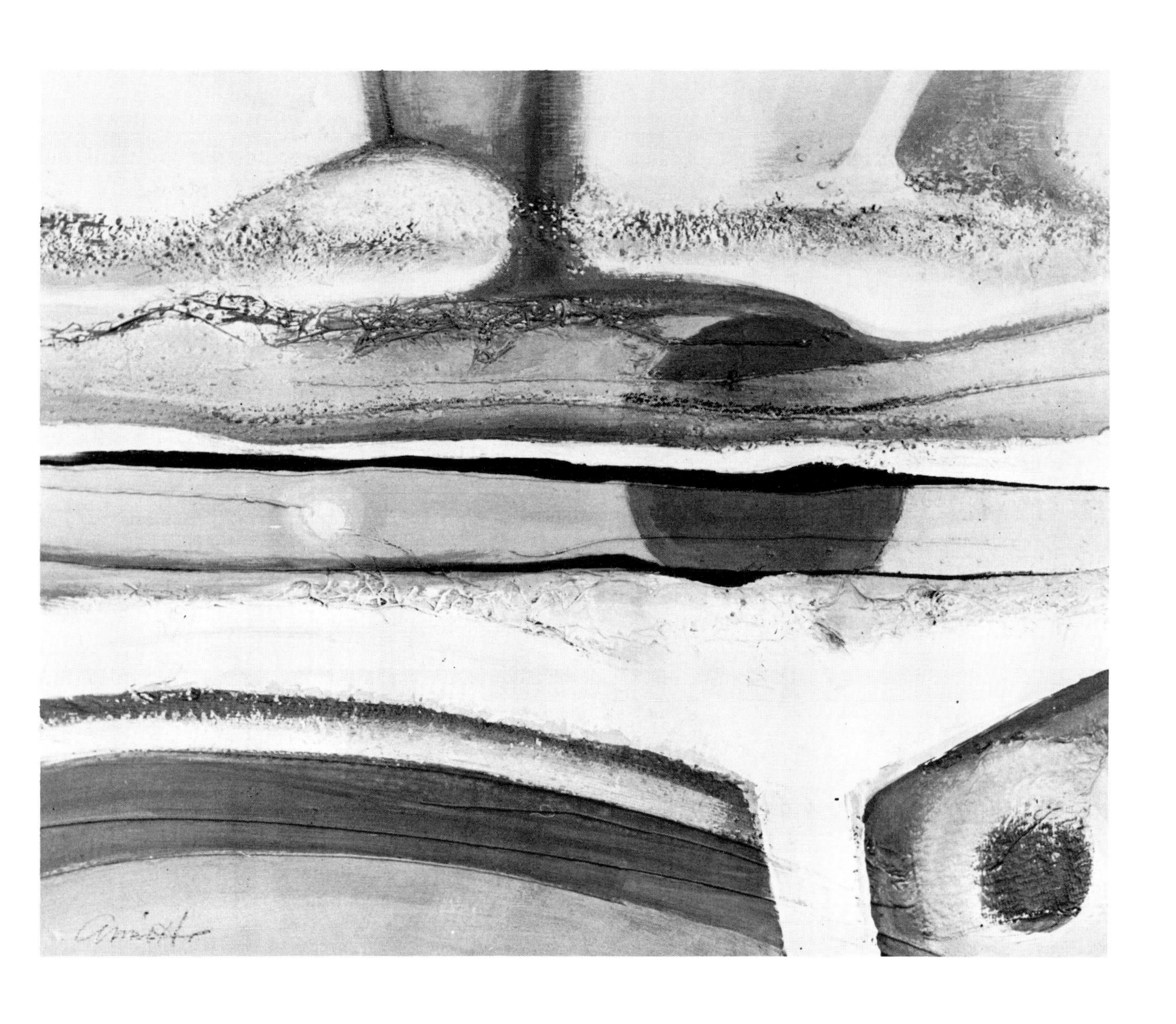

25 AMIOTTE: *Two Suns.* (1969). Casein, gravel, and fabric collage on masonite, 23 7/8 x 30". (69.22.2)

ROBERT PENN

WICANHPI: Star. Tribal band: Brule. Born Omaha, Nebraska, 1947 (mother, Brule Sioux from Rosebud Reservation, South Dakota; father, Omaha from Omaha Reservation, Nebraska). Attended St. Augustine Mission school, Winnebago, Nebraska; St. Francis High School, South Dakota, 1963-66; attended workshop in Contemporary Indian Art presented by Oscar Howe at University of South Dakota, Vermillion, summer 1966; studying creative arts at University of South Dakota, Vermillion, South Dakota, 1966 to present. Lives Vermillion, South Dakota.

"Despite all the tribulations of the world today, a sure sign that man is not doomed to imminent destruction and decay is the fresh insight into today's art. Modern art, if you will! This is regional in the sense that it grows from a particular soil native to the artist. It is international, as all art is, in the sense that it is made by man. For the first time, artists all over the world can be a part of it. No matter how different man may be from one another, art is a common reminder of the common origins. I feel it is a function of art to be a reconciling force, to find interrelations between seemingly separate objects and events, to dissolve causes of opposition, and to give a meeting ground for different heritages. Art tells a stranger that he is not so strange – nor is he alone."

– Robert Penn

Opposite page.
26 PENN: *Untitled.* (1969). Oil on canvas, 52½ x 38¼". (69.23.42)

27 PENN: *Tipi.* (1969). Oil on canvas, 39 1/8 x 35¼". (69.23.39)

28 PENN: *Skin Painting.* (1969). Oil on canvas, 27 5/8 x 28½". (69.23.40)

EARL EDER

TANCAN HANSKA: Longchasie. Tribal band: Yanktonai. Born Poplar, Montana, on the Fort Peck Reservation, 1944. Attended public schools in Poplar, Montana; studied art at Institute of American Indian Arts, Santa Fe, New Mexico, 1962-66; studying painting at San Francisco Art Institute, California, 1967 to present. Lives in San Francisco, California.

"I always knew I was going to be an artist; but I did not find myself and I am still searching."

— *Earl Eder.*

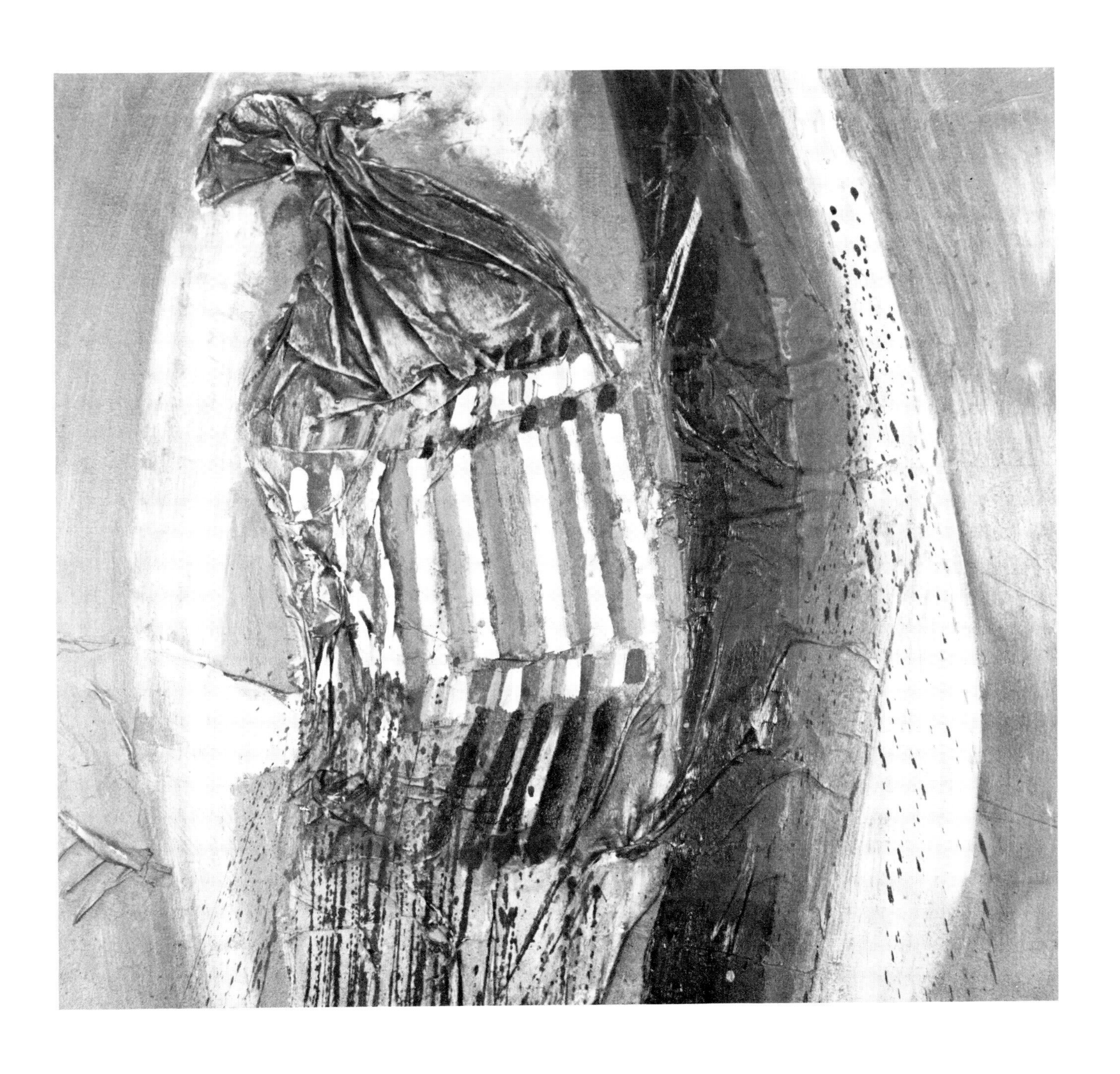

29 EDER: *A Sioux Bag.* (1965). Oil and paper collage on canvas, 26 5/8 x 30". (69.18.12)

AUSTIN RAVE

WAWE HAKTA: Cares For His People. Tribal band: Miniconjou. Born on the Cheyenne River Reservation, South Dakota, 1946, (mother, Miniconjou Sioux; father, Winnebago). Attended public schools, Eagle Butte, South Dakota; studied art at Institute of American Indian Arts, Santa Fe, New Mexico 1964-66; studied painting at San Francisco Art Institute, California, 1966. Awarded Governor's Trophy at Scottsdale National Indian Art Exhibition, 1966. Lives San Francisco, California.

30 RAVE: *Scout Signal.* 1965. Oil on canvas, 36 x 36". (69.18.4)

DUANE LAFFERTY

Tribal band: Oglala. Born Pine Ridge, South Dakota on the Pine Ridge Reservation, 1947. Attended Day School, Kyle, South Dakota; Oglala Community High School, Pine Ridge, South Dakota, 1964-65; studied painting at Institute of American Indian Arts, Santa Fe, New Mexico, 1966-68; attending National College of Business, Rapid City, South Dakota, 1969 to present. Lives in Rapid City, South Dakota.

31 LAFFERTY: *War Shield.* 1968. Oil and fabric collage on canvas, 24 x 48". (69.18.10)

DONALD MONTILEAUX

Tribal band: Oglala. Born Pine Ridge, South Dakota on the Pine Ridge Reservation, 1948. Attended Cathedral School, Rapid City, South Dakota; Rapid City High School, 1963-66; studied painting at Institute of American Indian Arts, Santa Fe, New Mexico, 1966-68; Black Hills State College, Spearfish, South Dakota, 1970 to present. Lives in Spearfish, South Dakota.

"I look forward to some day of having my art work recognized as being outstanding. It is really a thrill to have a painting accepted for any special art exhibition. I have enjoyed studying at the Institute of American Indian Art. I plan to continue my art education."
– Don Montileaux.

32 MONTILEAUX: *Untitled.* (1968). Oil on canvas, 57 x 31 7/8". (68.24.4)

SUGGESTED READINGS

ALEXANDER, HARTLEY BURR
Sioux Indian Painting. 2 vols. Nice, France, C. Szwedzicki, 1938.

BARBEAU, MARIUS
Indian Days on the Western Prairies. Ottawa, 1960. (National Museum of Canada. Bulletin No. 163. Anthropological Series No. 46)

BLISH, HELEN H.
A Pictographic History of the Oglala Sioux, Drawings by Amos Bad Heart Bull. Lincoln, University of Nebraska Press, 1967.

DOCKSTADER, FREDERICK J.
Indian Art in America. Greenwich, Connecticut, New York Graphic Society, 1961.

DOUGLAS, FREDERICK H. AND RENE d'HARNONCOURT
Indian Art of the United States, an exhibition organized by the Indian Arts and Crafts Board of the U.S. Department of the Interior. New York, The Museum of Modern Art, 1941.

DUNN, DOROTHY
American Indian Painting of the Southwest and Plains Areas. Albuquerque, University of New Mexico Press, 1968.

EWERS, JOHN C.
Plains Indian Painting. Stanford University, California, Stanford University Press, 1939.

FEDER, NORMAN
North American Indian Painting. New York, The Museum of Primitive Art, 1967.

HASSRICK, ROYAL B., In Collaboration With DOROTHY MAXWELL and CILE M. BACH
The Sioux, Life and Customs of a Warrior Society. Norman, University of Oklahoma Press, 1964. (The Civilization of the American Indian Series)

HOWARD, JAMES H.
The Dakota or Sioux Indians, a Study in Human Ecology. Vermillion, South Dakota, 1966. (University of South Dakota, The Dakota Museum. Anthropological Papers, No. 2)

HOWARD, JAMES H.
The Warrior Who Killed Custer, the Personal Narrative of Chief Joseph White Bull. Lincoln, University of Nebraska Press, 1968.

LIBHART, MYLES
The Dance in Contemporary American Indian Art, an exhibition organized by the Indian Arts and Crafts Board of the U.S. Department of the Interior. New York, Harkness House for Ballet Arts, Gallery of the Dance, 1967.

MALLERY, GARRICK
Pictographs of the North American Indians. Washington, D.C., 1886. (Bureau of American Ethnology. Annual Report IV.)

MALLERY, GARRICK
Picture-writing of the American Indians. Washington, D.C., 1893. (Bureau of American Ethnology. Annual Report X.)

NEW, LLOYD
Institute of American Indian Arts. Washington, D.C., 1969. (U.S. Department of the Interior, Indian Arts and Crafts Board. Native American Arts, No. 1)

PENNINGTON, ROBERT
Oscar Howe, Artist of the Sioux. Sioux Falls, South Dakota, Dakota Territorial Centennial Commission, 1961.

SNODGRASS, JEANNE O.
American Indian Painters, A Biographical Directory. New York, 1968. (Contributions from the Museum of the American Indian, Heye Foundation. Vol. XXI, Part I)